The *Lesbian Couple's*

GUIDE TO WEDDING PLANNING

Dedication

*For Jen and Patrick, Team Coveney Smith
always and forever.*

Published by Sellers Publishing, Inc.
161 John Roberts Road, South Portland, Maine 04106

Visit our Web site: sellerspublishing.com • E-mail: rsp@rsvp.com

The Lesbian Couple's Guide to Wedding Planning has been adapted, revised, and
updated from the author's self-published book, *Gay Wedding Confidential*.

ISBN: 978-1-4162-0914-0
e-ISBN: 978-1-4162-0958-4

Library of Congress Control Number: 2013931256

10 9 8 7 6 5 4 3 2 1

Printed and bound in China.

Everything you need to know about
planning your dream wedding

The *Lesbian Couple's*
GUIDE TO WEDDING PLANNING

by Bernadette Coveney Smith

Advice from America's #1 Same-Sex Wedding Expert

Photographs by Katje Hempel

SELLERS
PUBLISHING

Contents

Introduction

Like many LGBT Americans on election day 2012, I was sitting anxiously on the edge of my seat, eagerly awaiting not only the presidential election results but also the results of the four ballot initiatives that had an effect on same-sex marriage. Would the voters say yes or, like dozens of times before, refuse to support marriage equality? I was cautiously optimistic, but even this gay-wedding planner didn't expect such a resounding 4/4 victory!

Voters in Maryland, Maine, and Washington affirmed marriage equality, and their support allowed same-sex marriage laws to go into effect. And voters in Minnesota refused to allow a discriminatory anti-gay marriage law to pass. These historic wins told us, the times, they are a-changin', and it was an absolutely exhilarating night.

I'm sure many same-sex couples are now rushing off to the altar as a result of those victories. For me personally, election night 2012 was reminiscent of another historic time nine years earlier.

On November 18, 2003, I was driving in my car, listening to National Public Radio. A news bulletin indicated that, later that day, a decision in the case of *Goodridge* v. *the Massachusetts Department of Public Health* would be reached. This lawsuit was filed to remove the state's ban on same-sex marriage. At the time, I had just come back to Boston from a Caribbean holiday with my girlfriend, and I was overcome with excitement to hear what this momentous decision would be.

I went to the office and glued myself to the Internet (constantly refreshing the screen!), waiting for the decision to be announced. Sometime around 11:00 a.m., in my cramped little office with a view of the brick wall of the building across the street, I heard the news that the state could no longer "deny the protections, benefits, and obligations conferred by civil marriage to two individuals of the same sex who wish to marry."

The decision stated that marriages between same-sex partners would take effect in six months, on May 17, 2004. Can you imagine the excitement? At the time, the Netherlands was one of the few places in the world that let gay and lesbian couples legally marry. Our neighbor, Vermont, permitted something odd called "civil unions," which were separate from, and unequal to, a legal marriage. But same-sex marriage was legal here in Massachusetts! It was historic and I was over the moon. We all were.

In March of that year, I decided to start my own LGBT wedding-planning company, It's About Time, and in May — one day after same-sex marriage went into effect in Massachusetts, I got a call from a gay couple for my first assignment — to plan their wedding *in just six days!*

A wedding in a week. They had the venue — a historic church. I needed to find someone to bake the wedding cake, a photographer, flowers, an organist, and ingredients for enough punch to serve to a large crowd at the reception immediately following the ceremony — the wedding and reception were open to all church members.

The ceremony was at First Church Boston, a Unitarian Universalist church that performs same-sex marriages. One of the grooms was so excited that his was going to be the first same-sex wedding at this historic church that he wrote and distributed a press release. The couple took care of renting their tuxes and making reservations for the dinner after the reception, but the bulk of the planning was up to me.

Within those six days, I hired vendors with whom I would later work routinely. The ceremony was very elegant, and the grooms were stunningly handsome in their sharp black tuxes with their calla lily boutonnieres. All the vendors stepped up and did their jobs exceptionally well. My girlfriend at the time and I cooked up a delicious punch concoction in the church's kitchen, which we served along with wedding cake to the guests, some of whom were perfect strangers to the grooms.

That day, I learned such skills as when and how to unroll an aisle runner, how to line up the members of the wedding party, and when to cue the organist for the processional.

I also discovered the pure joy of same-sex weddings — the feeling of extreme jubilation that is present among the guests. There's a feeling of anticipation, since many guests have never been to a same-sex wedding before. That's followed by an inevitable lack of dry eyes during the ceremony because the sense of history in the room is unmistakable. The guests just know they are a part of something bigger than themselves.

There's no question: LGBT weddings just feel different from heterosexual weddings. Every same-sex wedding is still making history. The guests at these weddings might not know it at the time, but each same-sex wedding helps to change the world, one beautiful marriage at a time, creating a powerful ripple effect that spreads to curious co-workers, neighbors, and friends who are often moved by the pure, simple power of love.

Fast-forward six years — a couple traveled to Cambridge from New York (before same-sex marriage was legal there) to get married. I picked them up at their hotel in the morning and brought them to Cambridge City Hall to apply for their license. After that, I went with them to apply for a "marriage without delay" waiver at the courthouse, and when that was granted, we returned to City Hall to pick up their license.

All the while, I heard great stories about their families and their jobs, and an adorable account of how they met. (One of my favorite parts of wedding planning is getting a glimpse into the lives of incredible individuals, as I become familiar with their relatives, their stories, and their tastes.)

But the best part of the day (I think we'd all agree) was when we were in Cambridge City Hall, license in hand, with the Honorable Denise Simmons (justice of the peace and, at that time, mayor of Cambridge). She officiated a beautiful, simple ceremony in her office, and at its conclusion, she presented my clients with a felt bag. Inside it was a key to the city of Cambridge.

Imagine the reaction of these two ladies! They were elated! I didn't know it was coming — but what a wonderful surprise it was for all of us! I've worked with Ms. Simmons a number of other times after that, and she always does a wonderful job, but that occasion was particularly special. I feel that every time our team brings our clients to Cambridge, we are treating them to a little piece of LGBT history.

In the nine years since that ruling, I have planned many weddings for a wide variety of fascinating couples, and I'll share some of their stories throughout the book. In those nine years, I also got married myself, had a son, and last year, moved from Massachusetts to New York (though we are still open for business in Massachusetts).

When I was asked to write a book specifically for the lesbian bride (though some of you may prefer the term "bridegroom"), I was excited to fill a void. A book like this simply doesn't exist — yet the interests of lesbians *are* different from those of gay men. After all, gay men (usually) don't need to know a thing about shopping for a wedding gown! Lesbians wonder how to deal with two mothers of the brides and how to express themselves through their wedding attire. Having worked with hundreds of lesbian couples, I've realized that we have our own needs, our own agendas, our own music — and our own wedding tastes and concepts. And now, finally, we have our very own lesbian wedding-planning guide.

This book is written for anyone who's planning a wedding, but especially those who are, like me, lesbians. For the purpose of keeping things simple, I typically use the terms "lesbian," "brides," "same-sex," and "LGBT" when referring to our community, and "brides" when referring to the wedding couple. I know some of you are transgender and some lesbians don't identify as brides — but I'm not trying to be exclusive, I promise! As you read the book, you'll see I've highlighted special tips that may be helpful for transgender brides or grooms.

Thank you for reading this book. I wish you all the best in your journey together as a couple and with your wedding plans. I'm hopeful that my candid and practical approach will give you the tools you need to create a wonderful wedding that reflects your personality and love for one another.

Enjoy!

Chapter 1
Beginnings

My Beginnings

Here's my story: I had my very own lesbian wedding on July 3, 2009, in downtown Boston on Boston Harbor. I married the love of my life, Jennifer Coveney. She's beautiful! (See our wedding photo on the opposite page — I'm on the left and Jen is on the right.) We met about two years prior, at a bar, and it was a love-at-first-sight kind of moment. That day was Jennifer's first at a new job in Connecticut. She had returned to Boston that night to go out with friends, and as fate would have it, I was there.

We had a whirlwind romance as many lesbian couples do, and within nine months, she had quit her job in Connecticut, took another in Boston, and moved in with me. Have you heard the second-date joke?

What does a lesbian bring to her second date?

A U-Haul!

That was us, *almost!*

Before Jen moved back to Boston, however, we'd been talking about marriage for a few months and knew that we were completely perfect for each other. We had had conversations about engagement ring styles, and I had a sense of what she wanted. I even had an image printed off the Internet of the kind of ring she liked. One day, I decided that, just for kicks, I'd go ring shopping in downtown Boston, and get a sense of what the cost might be and how difficult it would be to find the style she liked. (It should be noted that this is one of the parts of planning a wedding I'd never been involved in, since my clients almost always have the ring when I meet them! Prior to my turn, I'd never been ring shopping.)

The second store I went to had the setting (which was a hybrid-tension setting) in stock, and the salesman showed me some diamond options. Before I knew it, I had committed to buying a ring. It happened quickly and easily, much more so than I had expected. During the week that the ring was being cut and set, I cooked up a number of elaborate and clever ways to propose. I was full of brilliant ideas, but when I picked the ring up, I buried it in the back of my file cabinet and tried not to think about it — I wanted to wait a few months.

A few weeks later, Jen moved in. That Sunday night, I made dinner (and it was appallingly bad). We were sitting in our pajamas, looking adoringly at each other, when Jen took my hand and said, "I can't imagine being any happier than I am at this moment." I'm not sure what came over me — I think I saw her statement as a challenge — but I politely excused myself to "get a sweater." I returned with the ring, mumbled something sweet, and before I knew it, we were engaged and out at our favorite restaurant for strawberry shortcake and Champagne.

Everyone has a different story, and it's been fun watching my own unfold while working with others. As I said before, one of my favorite parts of being an LGBT wedding planner is getting to know all kinds of couples and catching glimpses of their lives. I've worked with couples who've been together for 30 years, dwelling in the suburbs; couples who have kids and reside on a quiet urban neighborhood street; couples who live in a downtown loft; and many couples who, like me and Jen, experienced love at first sight and didn't want to wait to begin the fun part of being together forever.

Your Beginnings: Who Proposes and Who Gets the Ring?

Common question: *With lesbian couples, does the person who gets proposed to have to "propose back" with a ring?*

As far as I'm concerned there's no right answer about who proposes, who gets a ring, and what that ring looks like.

If you and your partner are talking about marriage, don't be afraid to have a conversation about the ring. It's better to know what your partner likes so you can be prepared. I've noticed that many lesbian couples don't want a "rock" — a big diamond engagement ring. I've seen femme lesbians present their butch partner with cuff links instead of an engagement ring!

I've found that younger lesbian brides (those under 40) are likelier to wear two rings. For example, my wife Jen wears her engagement ring and her wedding band next to each other on the same finger. This is very common and, of course, traditional. My engagement ring doesn't have a stone (my choice), so I wear it on the ring finger of my right hand; my wedding band is on the ring finger of my left hand.

In many cases, lesbian couples have been together for so many years that they already own rings that symbolize the permanence of their relationship, and those are the rings that they will continue to wear after their marriage. Conversely, a number of couples who have been wearing rings that reflect their commitment to each other choose to pick out new wedding bands together — bands that symbolize the next chapter in their lifetime journey. In my experience, couples who've been together for a while are less likely to have had a traditional "pop the question" proposal experience, and hence they don't buy or give engagement rings.

So, while there is no standard "lesbian engagement ring" or "lesbian wedding band," this can be one of the first areas where you as a couple can express your personality through your wedding.

"What If I Don't Feel like a Bride?"

There are a lot of you reading this book who probably don't think of yourselves in terms of being a bride. You may want to wear a suit or tux. You may identify as butch, boyish, queer, or trans. You may want to wait at the end of the aisle for your bride to

arrive for the ceremony. Or none of the above. The fact of the matter is, you just don't feel like a bride. What should we call you?

I personally use the term "bridegroom," and my clients seem to like it since it's kind of a queer term and has an old-school meaning. I know others who use the term "broom." Go with whatever you want. But if you do have a preference, be sure to speak up to the professionals involved in your wedding!

A Marriage or a Wedding?

Since 2004, there have been about 80,000 same-sex marriages in those states in the United States where it's been legal. During the six months that same-sex marriage was legal in California, there were 18,000 same-sex marriages! That's a lot for sure, but I know for certain that many of those couples had a simple marriage ceremony, not a big wedding. I met a couple recently that, like many others, had a brief marriage at the Unitarian Universalist Arlington Street Church during the first week that same-sex marriages were legal in Massachusetts. At that point, the church was holding marriage ceremonies every 15 minutes.

My company provides wedding-planning services — but it also provides marriage-planning services for those who simply want to make it legal. Which fits your style — an intimate marriage or a wedding with lots of family and friends in attendance? Whatever you choose, there's a good reason for each.

I've seen the "marriage versus wedding" debate arise among couples, especially those who grew up thinking it would never be possible to marry, or who've never envisioned their own wedding. I've met many couples who are unsure whether they want a wedding; in some circumstances, one partner is trying to convince the other on the subject.

In the beginning, back in 2004, many couples I worked with were in their 40s and 50s, and there was enormous pent-up demand for the legal right to marry. Some of those couples rushed to marry right away because they were afraid the legal right was going to be taken away, as it has been in other states since.

Now that same-sex marriage is secure in a number of states in the United States, it's become normalized in those places as the next logical step in a relationship, just as it is with our straight counterparts.

So, what do you do: have an intimate marriage ceremony or a big wedding? Jen and I can relate. We were talking about this topic when discussing how our wedding planning would have gone if I hadn't been a wedding planner. She said that she would have tried to convince me to have an elopement; just the two of us. I said that, even if I hadn't been a planner, I would never have gone along with that: having my friends and family witness and validate my marriage was way too important to me.

I have a lot of experience with weddings, and there is nothing more moving to me, still to this day, than seeing a gay or lesbian couple stand up in front of their friends and family and get legally married. The validation and support they receive from their guests is truly priceless. The key word is *validation*. LGBT weddings are jubilant. There is a sense of triumph. And there is no greater party.

Of course, weddings cost a lot of money, with the national average being $28,000, depending of course on the number of guests. For many people, that's the deciding factor on whether to elope or have a big wedding. I understand the desire to elope or to keep the event small. Many brides don't like being the center of attention or simply can't or don't want to spend the money or deal with the planning stress. And I'll never try to convince a couple otherwise. The validation of one's community that I needed isn't something everyone needs.

"What's Normal?"

Two of the questions I often get from couples and clients (and reporters and anyone curious about same-sex weddings) are, "What's normal?" and "What does a same-sex wedding look like?" In fact, to address these questions, I developed one seminar for engaged same-sex couples and another for professionals in the wedding industry hoping to work with the LGBT community — and, of course, it's one of the main reasons I felt the need to write this book!

Every time that same-sex marriage becomes legal in a new place, these questions arise over and over. Couples never expected the day would come and don't know what to do to prepare or how to make their wedding special. In fact, I went to an event recently where I heard a story of an Iowa couple who came to Massachusetts to get married one week before the ruling legalizing same-sex marriage in Iowa was issued. I know that, when many same-sex couples in Iowa began applying for their marriage licenses, they were thinking, "Now what? How the heck do I plan an LGBT wedding?"

Any wedding, gay or straight, should be about the personality and style of the couple. Don't let anyone tell you differently. The fundamental decisions are the same regardless of the couple's orientation. You have to think about how much to spend, whom to invite, what kind of celebration to have, and where to have it.

The Inevitable Wedding Stress

Wedding planning can wreak emotional havoc. Even when you're a wedding planner! (Perhaps *especially* when you're a wedding planner!) Throughout our engagement, it became increasingly odd for me to be on the other side of wedding planning and to go through so many of the same issues that my clients face. My concerns and emotions were not issues specific to an LGBT wedding; rather, they were issues any couple may go through.

My parents passed away over 12 years ago, so the planning was always a little bitter-sweet for me. Jen's mom came to town to go dress shopping with her. That's a timeless

rite of passage, and I relied on the kindness of my friends to share it with me (once I finally figured out what to wear).

All of my family lives out of state or out of the country, so only those in my immediate family were invited to our bridal shower, and from that short list only my sister actually came. Jen's family, on the other hand, lives mostly in Massachusetts, so our shower guests were mostly friends and Jen's family. My sister can hold her own and I was grateful that she was there, but it made me sad that she came alone. It also makes me enormously grateful to be blessed with amazing friends and for marrying into a family that completely embraces and supports me.

Like many brides, I was anxious about who from my Irish-Catholic family would come to the wedding. I invited dozens of cousins, aunts, and uncles from around the world, but I had zero sense as to who would actually make the trip to Boston for my lesbian wedding. When it was all said and done, I was lucky to have had great representation from both sides of my family — but the anticipation was a killer.

The Challenge in Coming Out

A wedding averages 43 different vendors, everyone from the hair and makeup artists, to the limo driver, to the coat-check guy. And when you, as a lesbian couple, are planning your wedding, you have to come out over and over and over again — to all of these people, both those whom you hire and even those whom you do not. Every time you visit a venue or taste a cake, you must come out. Every time you interview a florist or a wedding planner, you must come out. This could mean coming out 100-plus times over the course of planning your wedding. And unfortunately, in many places (over half of the U.S. states), it's legal for vendors to say, "I can't help you. I don't do lesbian weddings."

In the following states, vendors can legally discriminate against you: Alabama, Alaska, Arizona, Arkansas, Florida, Georgia, Idaho, Indiana, Kansas, Kentucky, Louisiana, Minnesota, Mississippi, Missouri, Montana, Nebraska, North Carolina, North Dakota, Ohio, Oklahoma, Pennsylvania, South Carolina, South Dakota, Tennessee, Texas, Utah, Virginia, West Virginia, and Wyoming.

Transgender Tip: Five states — Wisconsin, New Hampshire, Maryland, New York, and Delaware — have laws banning discrimination based on sexual orientation, but they do not explicitly include gender identity in their nondiscrimination policy, so you should be cautious.

Of course, every vendor my company works with is going to be great, but I know that there are other vendors that won't be as hospitable. If you are two women, when you enter a store you will encounter vendors who will ask, "Who's the bride?" even if they are lesbian-friendly.

Now, a situation like that doesn't always equal discrimination. Sometimes, it's just plain ignorance. It's up to you to decide whether to be offended. Ultimately, I believe in being preemptive and speaking up right from the beginning. If being vocal early on reduces stress later, then go for it. Here's how you should come out when speaking on the phone with a potential vendor: "Hi, I'm getting married to my partner Jen.

She proposed recently, and I want to inquire about your venue to host our lesbian wedding."

A FEW TIPS:

- Be proactive in coming out. Come out right away before vendors can make any assumptions about your sexual orientation.
- Trust your instincts. If there's any awkwardness or discomfort with whomever you are talking to, call someone else. There's another vendor who would love to work with you.
- Don't be afraid to ask the vendor about his or her experience with same-sex weddings.
- Don't be too quick to dismiss a vendor if he or she doesn't have any experience with LGBT weddings, but seems like a nice and supportive person. You may help a worthy vendor grow his or her business.

Note that I used the phrase "lesbian wedding" in the paragraph above about how to come out on the phone. Let there be no mistake that you are having a same-sex wedding when communicating with vendors. Some names are gender-ambiguous. Some vendors are clueless. Be clear from the get-go. If you are sending an e-mail message, being explicit about the fact that you're planning a same-sex wedding will (hopefully) minimize any accidental use of "bride and groom" in the vendor's canned e-mail response.

TRANSGENDER TIP: Coming out prior to meeting with a vendor is especially important if you are a transgender person. You don't want the vendor you meet with to have any misunderstandings during your in-person meeting.

I need to be honest and let you know that there's a good chance you're going to encounter some heterosexism and possibly homophobia, even if you're marrying in a state where same-sex marriage is legal. I want to tell you this because, even as a planner, I've seen some ugly things, even with vendors I had prescreened.

Here are some examples:

- I was invited to do a presentation to a group of wedding professionals on how to work with LGBT couples, and one of the vendors in the audience blatantly told me upon my arrival that she didn't work with same-sex couples and instead referred them to a colleague.

- I booked a trolley (from a company I'd used before) for my clients' wedding guests, and the man who helped me with my reservation asked me, "Which way do they swing?" when I told him it was a same-sex wedding.

- At another wedding, the trolley driver told me he couldn't wait to see the bride and groom. I reminded him there were two brides. The driver rolled his eyes and blessed himself.

I am not telling you these things to freak you out, to deter you from planning a fabulous wedding, or to scare you into hiring me or another same-sex wedding planner. Not at all. However, there's a misconception that all vendors are on board, accepting, and understanding because lesbian weddings have been happening in some places for several years now. But discrimination still exists. At least in the above situations, my clients didn't have to experience it themselves.

As you do your wedding-planning homework online and start to identify vendors, you'll stumble upon a number of online LGBT wedding directories, including:

- AVoteandaVow.com
- EnGAYgedweddings.com
- EquallyWed.com
- GayWeddings.com
- Gay.Weddings.com
- PurpleUnions.com
- RainbowWeddingNetwork.com

Many of these sites are "pay for play," which means that a wedding vendor can advertise on them without providing any validation or proof that they are, in fact, LGBT-friendly. The other sites will allow vendors to sign up for free listings without a thorough background check or screening process. Accordingly, I again recommend that, when you call a vendor, *any vendor, anywhere*, no matter who's referred them to you, you should come out right away and make no mistake about the fact that you're planning a lesbian wedding.

Bridezillas!

I am hereby giving you permission to be a bridezilla! I look at it this way: you're probably spending thousands of dollars on your wedding day. You want it to be perfect. You want to do this only once.

As you plan the big day, there are sure to be lots of stressors: moms or future mothers-in-law who have strong opinions (and may be paying for a portion of the wedding) or dear friends who themselves are showing 'zilla tendencies and need a lot of extra attention. You may suddenly have extra pressure at work. You may want to lose weight for the wedding. You may be very upset by your wedding gown alterations (Jen knows all about this one . . .) or experience difficulty buying a suit (I know all about that one . . .). So be a 'zilla if you feel like it. Most of us in the wedding industry don't mind. And we know better than to take it personally.

Honestly, I understand, and Jen and I have each had our own 'zilla moments in the course of planning our own wedding. Weddings are stressful and get many people around you excited. You are probably going to get lots of unsolicited advice and opinions, and if you are a lesbian couple, you're probably going to get lots of advice from straight friends and family who will tell you how a wedding *should* look and feel based on their own experiences with straight weddings.

Stand your ground. It's *your* wedding, and *your* vision. I'd hate for you to lose sight of that, and to lose part of your identity in the process (even if this means that you sometimes act like a 'zilla). You don't have to apologize for it. At some point in every planning process, I hear from one partner, "I'm sorry, I'm having a 'zilla moment" or "I went *so* 'zilla on my mother last night." I'd much rather have that happen than have a couple upset that their vision has been compromised. If you were my client, I'd take it all in stride.

Rock on, 'zillas!

Chapter 2
Getting Started

Sharing your news with family
Planning a kid-friendly wedding

✔ Sharing Your News with Family

Your parents may be thrilled for you when you announce that you're marrying a person of the same gender, but keep in mind that some parents will freak out. I've seen my share of both situations and have talked with numerous couples for whom the parental reaction is a big stressor. One of my clients related:

> *My mom seemed to be really trying to prepare us for the possibility that my dad wouldn't be coming to the wedding. He didn't talk about it and didn't acknowledge it at all while we were there this weekend, and when she tries to make plans he says he doesn't want to talk about it. My take on it is that we will have a beautiful, memorable wedding with or without him, and I'm going to put all my focus and energy into enjoying the rest of our planning and getting excited for the big day.*

But this isn't a chapter about coming out to your parents or dealing with their acceptance or rejection. Chances are you've already done that. I'm not here to talk about religion or politics. I'm here to talk about getting your parents *excited* for your lesbian wedding!

Some parents have a hard time with the idea of same-sex marriage, even if they support your relationship. To some, a same-sex marriage may not seem real because it may not be sanctioned in the state where they live. And if you're like me and Jen and some of our clients, the relationship may have been a whirlwind one and the engagement may have come fairly quickly. In fact, Jen waited a few weeks to tell her parents that we were engaged because she didn't want them to be appalled by how quickly it all happened.

Whatever the case, the question is, how do you get your parents excited about your same-sex wedding? In our own situation, when Jen ultimately shared the news, she did not get the reaction she had hoped for from her parents. They were a bit stunned. In all fairness, Jen had been engaged to a woman before (in her wild youth), but now she was a grown-up, in her 30s, and she had found me. (And I'm very lovable!) But her parents were less than thrilled. Why?

I've talked to Jen's parents about their ambivalence, and a large part of their feelings were related to the fact that, as Maryland residents, same-sex marriage wasn't on their radar. It didn't seem possible to them. Yet in Massachusetts, where we lived at the time, it was a reality. We were used to it. They were not.

The Seven Steps to Dealing with Your Parents

STEP ONE: BE PATIENT

Don't get bent out of shape if your parents are less enthusiastic than you'd hoped. Give them time. Don't get defensive and bitter. Remember that it may have taken you a while to get used to the idea of being lesbian or of getting married, so be patient with their process. Your parents may feel like your wedding plans are a runaway train. They may feel like you got engaged out of the blue, and are furiously planning this big event, while they're left at the station wondering what the heck just happened. I recall Jen, being frustrated and angry with her parents for not being more excited about our

wedding. I urged her to have patience. She had no choice. Jen's parents are incredibly kind people and came around, as we had hoped they would.

STEP TWO: SLOWLY SHARE YOUR EXCITEMENT

Gradually start sharing your excitement about the wedding plans. Say things like, "We took a look around at venues today and it was really fun," or "I've been looking through bridal magazines for dresses I might like." One that works great is, "I received the sweetest engagement card in the mail today from Aunt Mary! She sounds so excited for us!" My advice is to just say typical wedding-planning things, as if it's any other conversation with your parents. Don't make a big deal out of the plans at first, but start to plant the seed that your wedding is for real and that you are taking action. I urged Jen to slowly start releasing information about our ideas, just in the normal course of conversation. It piqued her mom's curiosity.

STEP THREE: ASK FOR ADVICE

Asking for advice, not financial help (at least not yet), is the most critical step. Ask open-ended questions about etiquette issues, like whom to invite. An example would be, "Should we invite all of our second cousins to the wedding?" Or ask for advice about logistical matters: "We're thinking of having an outdoor ceremony. What do you think of that?" You want to involve your parents without generating guilt.

STEP FOUR: INVITE GREATER PARTICIPATION

Over time, invite your parents to participate in more emotional wedding-planning issues. I believe that excitement is contagious, and if you are thrilled about your wedding, eventually your parents will be too. You'll know when the time is right to recruit them to be actively involved.

Shopping for a dress became a turning point for Jen in our wedding plans. This is where Jen's parents boarded the Coveney-Smith wedding train. Her mom came to town, and they went dress shopping. Jen started talking about the bridal shower. During her visit, Jen's mom visited the place where we were to marry and loved it. And when she went back home, she was filled with delight. Jen's dad then got enthusiastic, too, and the Coveney-Smith wedding train started to pull out of the station.

STEP FIVE: ASK FOR MONEY

If you need to ask for money, wait until your parents have become excited about the wedding and are sharing their ideas and etiquette advice. Obviously, do this only if your parents have some reasonable capacity to contribute. Use your best judgment. One of the easiest ways to broach the subject is to complain about money: "I didn't know how much a wedding was going to cost." And here's the best one: "I don't think we can invite the cousins, your friends from work, and/or your next-door neighbors, because we just can't afford it."

If your parents bite and are willing to contribute, I'd advise asking for a specific dollar amount, rather than for coverage of certain expenses. The reason is that, if you ask them to pay for the band and the photographer, your parents might feel like they get to select those vendors. And you don't want to relinquish that control. This is your vision.

If you don't feel comfortable making a specific "ask," go for the general hint. One of Jen's priceless gems was, "Even though Bernadette's a wedding planner, it's still crazy how much things cost when it's your own wedding!" Jen's parents were very generous.

STEP SIX: GIVE YOUR PARENTS A PROJECT
Channel your parents' new enthusiasm into a defined project. This is very important if you want to retain ownership of your wedding plans. The goal is to engage your parents with something they would strive to be good at. Moms often like being a hostess, so you might give one of them the project of planning the bridal shower or wedding-weekend activities for out-of-town guests. Another good project is to ask Mom to be in charge of hotel-welcome gift bags. Maybe your dad likes to make homemade beer or wine? If so, perhaps he can make favors for your guests.

STEP SEVEN: KEEP THE PROJECTS COMING
Parents like to feel that they're contributing. If your parents live out of state, and you can tell they're nervous when they come to town, have them channel that energy to your benefit. We had Jen's mom assembling out-of-town guest gift bags and writing out escort cards. We had her parents, her sister, and her sister's boyfriend come over

to our condo to help load up the car with decorations and tidy up our place. These "assignments" worked like a charm and everyone had fun with them

✔ Planning a Kid-Friendly Wedding

When thinking about whom to invite to your wedding, one of the "categories" is children. Initially, many of my clients were in their 40s and 50s and had been together for many years. It's common for such couples, having waited for decades for legal recognition of their relationship, to be homeowners and to have children. When that's the case, the wedding will simply not be a Saturday night dance party with the guests doing the "Electric Slide."

In one such instance, my clients Sue and Anne were doctors, and they had been together for 11 years and had three children. They wanted a festive, Sunday afternoon, interfaith family wedding — with 110 adults and 70 children! They lived in an adorable, pale-yellow house on a quiet street in a diverse Boston neighborhood, and the two littlest kids (twins, a boy and a girl) were still nursing. How do you plan a wedding where there will be 70 kids? This is not your average wedding challenge, but we hit the ground running to pull this one off.

This couple and I looked at many wedding venues, and I helped them choose one with a pond and a large, nicely landscaped lawn, providing ample space for the children to play, and to accommodate their substantial guest list in a tent. The floral designer created a gorgeous *chuppah* (wedding canopy) with a natural, curly-willow archway, and the ceremony was held near the pond. The interfaith ceremony was officiated by a rabbi, and the bridal processional included the partners' children.

Later, the band performed the traditional Jewish wedding dance, the *hora*, and lots of other family-friendly music. The caterer designed an entirely separate menu for the children, including a station for them during "mocktail hour." We hired a children's entertainer as well as someone to lead them in arts-and-crafts activities throughout the afternoon. The end result was a beautiful, naturally elegant wedding with something for everyone. The guests were entertained for hours.

I've planned many weddings for lesbian couples with children — or with children on the way — or where lots of children were welcome. You'll want to be sure to hire one or more babysitters who can provide toys and DVDs, for the younger children in particular. If you or the parents don't know of any babysitters, you can ask your wedding planner for suggestions. There are some national companies that provide sitters. One example is ElegantEventSitters.com. You may also have luck on SitterCity.com. As a last resort, call around to local daycare providers to see if they provide child care for special events.

There are some really creative ways to involve kids in the ceremony itself. If you do have one or more children, you can acknowledge them in your vows, or make a vow to the child/children. If you have a unity ritual, a third candle can represent the child/children. Your officiant can help you find the best way to incorporate kids into your wedding ceremony, should you choose to do so.

Chapter 3
Twelve Months Out

Create an organizing system
Plan your wedding budget/savings
Name your "besties" for the wedding party
Decide if you need a wedding planner
How to choose a wedding planner
How to let friends help if they offer

✔ Create an Organizing System

To keep things simple for you, this book is set up in a 12-month countdown format so you can see exactly which tasks and projects to tackle in the year leading up to your wedding. It's very important to have a system in place so you stay organized (and don't lose your mind!) through this very stressful wedding-planning process. A sensible, easy-to-use system is a must. As a wedding planner, I use online tools, as do most of my clients. I recommend such convenient — and "green" — options as Google. Docs, Dropbox.com, and Apple's iCloud to share your wedding-planning files and to keep in touch (and on schedule) with family, friends, and vendors.

✔ Plan Your Wedding Budget/Savings

When I work with a new client, one of the first things we do is to create a budget — a very specific, line-item budget. The one I use has two categories, variable expenses and fixed expenses. The cost of items under variable expenses (such as food) changes as the number of your wedding guests changes. The fixed expenses (such as photography) do not change as your guest count changes. You don't have to have a wedding planner to make a chart like the one that follows, which I created in Microsoft Excel. The "Per Person/Piece" column relates to variable expenses. Costs vary widely from region to region.

	PER PERSON/PIECE	ESTIMATED COST	ACTUAL COST
VARIABLE EXPENSES			
Save-the-date cards			
Postage			
Invitations			
Rehearsal dinner			
Welcome gifts			
Parking			
Coat check			
Ceremony program			
Food and service staff (assumes hors d'oeuvres and 3–4 course dinner)			
Alcohol and bar service (assuming full open bar)			
Admin fee + gratuity for food and beverage			
Cake			
Favors			
Place cards			
Subtotal A			

	PER PERSON/PIECE	ESTIMATED COST	ACTUAL COST
FIXED EXPENSES			
Hotel room			
Officiant fee			
Ceremony rental (if a house of worship)			
Ceremony and cocktail hour music (assuming trio)			
Transportation (assuming one limo all night)			
Bouquets (assuming 4 average size)			
Corsages/boutonnieres (assuming 8)			
Ceremony arrangements (assuming 2)			
Reception rental			
Wardrobe - partner A			
Wardrobe - partner B			
Wedding rings			
Hair and makeup			
Photographer - no albums			
Videographer			
Centerpieces			
Disc jockey			
Band			
Tent			
Dance floor			
Speciality linens			
Tables and chairs			
Place settings			
Lighting/other decorations			
Subtotal B			
Grand Total			

You may not be purchasing or renting everything on the above list. For example, you may choose a venue where the tables, chairs, tent, and the dance-floor rental are not necessary. This is simply a comprehensive list of wedding expenses so you can be fully informed of the possibilities.

Make a budget and stick to it, to the best of your ability!

Think a lot about your taste and style. If you have Abercrombie taste on an Old Navy budget, then you should invite fewer guests or have a destination wedding — or even elope! There are more tips in the chapters ahead on how to save money on your wedding.

✔ Name Your "Besties" for the Wedding Party

When it comes to selecting your wedding party, you've got a lot of categories that you could potentially fill — from best woman (or best man) to bridesmaids (or brides' mates) to maid (or person) of honor to attendants. Which of your "besties" will you want to include — all or some or none at all? This is one of those areas where I'll say "anything goes at a lesbian wedding." You can mix it up and have opposite-gender individuals as your attendants. You don't have to have any attendants at all. You can "share" attendants. Why not? This is a lesbian wedding and you can do whatever the heck you want. I'm not going to keep saying that, I promise. But you can. Over half of the weddings I've planned have not had wedding parties — and that's perfectly wonderful because it keeps the emphasis on the couple.

That said, if you *do* want a wedding party, you'll want to know what to expect from your attendant(s). (For the purpose of being gender-neutral and for ease of communicating, I'll be relying heavily on the word "attendant.")

My wife Jen and I had two girls on each side, four attendants in total. All but one were actually straight. The girls were in charge of invitations for — and activities at — the bridal shower. They also threw us a bachelorette party, but otherwise they didn't have a ton of responsibility. We asked them to wear navy but gave them complete freedom in their outfit selection. We didn't ask them to give toasts or to dance with one another.

Here are the traditional roles of members of a wedding party. You'll notice that they are typically given lots of responsibility:

Maid of Honor
- Goes dress and veil shopping with the bride
- Throws the bridal shower if a family member does not
- Helps assemble and mail invitations
- Attends the wedding rehearsal
- Has her hair and makeup done with the bride before the wedding
- Helps the bride to dress before the wedding
- Participates in the wedding processional
- Holds the groom's wedding ring
- Holds the bride's flowers
- Helps with the bustle after the ceremony
- Dances with the best man at the wedding reception

Best Man
- Throws a bachelor party
- Helps the groom choose a tuxedo
- Attends the wedding rehearsal
- Helps the groom get dressed before the wedding
- Participates in the wedding processional or waits at the altar with the groom and officiant
- Holds the bride's wedding ring

- Toasts the happy couple at the wedding reception

- Dances with the maid of honor at the wedding reception

- Returns any rental tuxedos

Bridesmaids
- Attend the shower

- Attend the wedding rehearsal

- Participate in the wedding processional

- Dance with groomsmen at the reception

Groomsmen
- Attend the bachelor party

- Seat wedding guests

- Attend the wedding rehearsal

- Unroll the wedding runner, if one is used

- Participate in the wedding processional, or wait at the altar with the groom and officiant

- Dance with bridesmaids at the wedding reception

Flower Girl
- Typically, flower girls are young, and not much is expected of them. They'll often carry a basket of flowers during the wedding processional. Sometimes, they will toss petals on the aisle runner during the processional.

Ring Bearer
- The little guy serving as the ring bearer usually isn't asked to do too much. He will often walk next to the flower girl during the processional while holding the pillow with the wedding rings. If you do have a ring bearer, there's a new product that's a great alternative to the traditional ring pillow. Paloma's Nest is a company that created the Original Ring Bearer Bowl, a ceramic bowl that can have your choice of wording. It's adorable and truly an heirloom wedding item. The bowls can be purchased at PalomasNest.com.

WEDDING PARTY FACTS AND TIPS

Keep in mind the following as you are discussing your own wedding party:

- It's okay if someone declines your request to be in your wedding party. Take into consideration that the person asked might have financial challenges, work issues, or some other reason for not being able to attend.

- Choose the people with whom you are closest!

- You don't have to feel obligated to ask someone to be your attendant just because you were in his or her wedding. (Not asking someone can be an emotional landmine — but it's your wedding and your decision to make.)

- You don't have to have the same number of attendants on either side. It doesn't have to be matchy-matchy. (You don't have to go out and make new best friends or invite people you'd rather not have, just for the sake of "symmetry.") I repeat: no symmetry required.

- Some people are not comfortable with gender roles associated with wedding tasks. You might want to check this out with the people you'd like to serve as your attendants.

- Someone other than the "best person" will often toast the couple at the reception.

- Many lesbian weddings don't have bachelorette parties or bridal showers.

- Many lesbian couples don't ask their attendants to dance with one another at the reception.

- Many lesbian couples don't expect all their female attendants to wear the same dress, if they are even asked to wear a dress at all (pantsuits may be preferred). For attendant dresses, I'm a fan of designers like J. Crew and Aria, where you can match the fabric in a variety of styles that flatter every figure.

- There are often no formal introductions at a lesbian wedding, or if there are, it's typically just the newlyweds.

In short, if you're planning a lesbian wedding, there's a good chance you'll be asking a lot less of your attendants than your straight counterparts would.

Who Pays for What?

Your attendants are responsible for their own wedding attire, travel expenses, and accommodations. If you are offering attendants certain opportunities (such as access to the hair and makeup artist), they would cover that cost themselves. On the other hand, if you require an attendant to do anything special (like be part of a spa day for the girls), then, as the host, you should cover that cost. You should also buy each attendant a thank-you gift.

✔ Decide If You Need a Wedding Planner

Okay, it's 12 months before your wedding and you need to hit the ground running! Which means you need to kick your planning skills into high gear! If this is something which doesn't come naturally to you, you may need a wedding planner.

Clearly, since I'm a wedding planner I'm completely biased. But if you can afford a wedding planner, he or she is worth the expense. Besides keeping you on track, if you think about all the times you have to come out when planning your wedding, you'll realize how nice it would be to have someone do that for you. Part of your planner's job is to make sure every vendor you meet is awesome to you, not discriminatory. You don't want to hear annoying things like, *"That's not what happens at a real wedding!"* and a good wedding planner should be able to keep that from happening.

⇒ POP QUIZ ⇐

Ask yourselves these questions to determine whether you need a wedding planner:

- Do you have one or more kids, a lot of friends, family, and hobbies, and/or not a lot of free time? Is it less than six months until your preferred wedding date and you still don't have anything of significance accomplished?

- Are you too overwhelmed to sort through the 770,000 wedding venues that showed up in a Google search, and are you annoyed that most of the venue photos show you images of people and food, not wedding spaces?

- Do you need someone to explain how much weddings cost, and help manage your budget and make sure you stick to it?

- Do you want to be sure that the vendors you hire are lesbian-friendly, reliable, trustworthy, and do beautiful work?

- Do you have a vision for your wedding, but don't know how to turn your ideas into reality (and need help convincing your fiancée that your ideas aren't that crazy)?

- Do you want to avoid the mistakes you've seen at other people's weddings — poor flow to the event, not enough people dancing, the wedding ending early, bad food, cheesy DJ, and more?

- Do you want to avoid questions like, "So, which one of you is the bride?" and "Where's the bride?" when you walk into a floral studio or venue appointment?

- Do you have etiquette questions, such as who to invite, what wording to use, how to deal with family issues, whether to invite kids, and more?

- Are you also planning to start a new job, move to a new home, have a baby, or otherwise experience huge life changes during the months prior to your wedding?

- Do you want to relax on your wedding day and avoid worries about the schedule, the flow, where to put the guestbook, and when to walk down the aisle(s)? Do you *not* want to be the one who has to deal with wondering if the DJ will be late?

- Do you want to enjoy your engagement and spend the months prior to your wedding in quality time with your fiancée, planning your honeymoon, picking out china, and otherwise daydreaming about blissful married life?

If you answered "yes" to at least three of the questions above, you should probably hire a wedding planner!

Wedding planners typically provide the following services. The price for each service will vary depending on the scope of their work and where you live.

FULL SERVICE

Full-service wedding planning is "soup-to-nuts" and includes everything from finding you a venue and LGBT-friendly vendors to sending you down the aisle (if you have an aisle, of course). Creating a day-of-wedding schedule and coordinating and being responsible for all setup and breakdown is part of this service. Full-service planning should include a customized wedding budget, timeline, and task lists. You might also get design services such as a floor-plan design, custom table designs, and sometimes even stationery design.

PARTIAL SERVICE

Planners providing partial service generally assume you have a venue but need help nailing down some final LGBT-friendly vendors, as well as coordinating all the day-of services.

EVENT DESIGNER

Event designers go beyond planning and bringing together all the vendors — they also come up with concepts and themes, colors, and artwork, all the things necessary to bring together a cohesive vision that matches your personal goals for your wedding. Event designers coordinate flowers, linens, lighting, furniture rentals, signage and stationery, signature cocktails, and all the other elements that go into the way your event will look and feel.

Note: Wedding planners may or may not offer event-design services. Some wedding planners have design skills and some just don't. Not all planners are designers and not all designers are planners. You should also be aware that some florists provide expanded services beyond just floral design, and can also offer to coordinate linens, furniture, and other items.

DAY-OF COORDINATION

Day-of coordination may be the name of this service, but month-of coordination is usually a more accurate description. This service is provided to couples that have done all the planning themselves but want to make sure their vision is perfectly executed.

Regardless of your decision about a wedding planner, I recommend that you hire a day-of coordinator. The following are the services that a good day-of coordinator should provide:

- Your coordinator should have a meeting with you both at the wedding venue to talk through the layout, flow, floor plan, décor elements, and more. This meeting ensures that all of you are on the same page.

- The coordinator should ask you a ton of questions, such as, "Where do you want the flowers to be moved to after the ceremony?" and "What do you want to do with the leftover cake?" Basically, they should inquire about details that you may never think about on your own.

- After meeting with you, your day-of coordinator should put together a day-of-wedding schedule, which is very detailed. It should outline the timing for formal photos and toasts, describe movement and flow, and have setup and breakdown tasks. This schedule should be for your review before it is distributed to all the vendors hired for the wedding.

- You should receive a list of final payments due, plus suggested tip amounts. As a wedding planner, one of the most commonly asked questions I get is about how much to tip everyone.

- Your day-of coordinator should also rehearse your wedding ceremony with you. We insist on doing this with our clients so everyone can stay calm on their actual wedding day.

- On your wedding day, coordinators generally arrive at least two hours early for setup and decoration tasks. They manage flow, bring you Champagne after your ceremony recessional, cue toasts, cue the photographer and the DJ or band for announcements, pin corsages, line up groups for formal photos, load up your car with gifts and leftover wedding cake, and generally make sure you are as relaxed as you can possibly be.

Note: If you decide you want to hire a day-of-wedding coordinator, please don't send him or her into a poorly planned wedding. Every wedding planner has a nightmare story of a day-of coordination couple that planned themselves a "hot mess" of a wedding where there were some major details missed. It's your day-of coordinator's role to alleviate stress, but not to fix your inadequate plans.

✔ How to Choose a Wedding Planner

First of all, you should know that not many wedding planners have experience with same-sex weddings. Most don't. That's okay as long as: (a) you're okay with it, and (b) your wedding planner is open minded and eager to help you. Taking that into consideration, remember these five simple things:

1. The planner must make you feel important. A planner's job is to be focused on the couple that he or she is with, not the couple getting married two days later. You must be comfortable with your planner and you must be made to feel special. If the planner does his or her job right, you may miss that person after the wedding because it was like you became old friends. And if you're unsure about whether you and your wedding are a priority, speak up immediately!

2. Trust is critical. You have to trust your planner with your vision but also with your heart. The reality is that you're entrusting your planner to come out for you and to connect you with the right vendors for the job — vendors who you, in turn, can trust. You don't want anyone with issues of homophobia or heterosexism on your wedding day.

3. Your wedding is your wedding — that's why I'm okay with bridezillas. You're the boss and your wedding shouldn't feel cookie-cutter to you. Your planner should understand your vision fully and should put as much effort as possible into bringing that vision to life. He or she acts as your representative to vendors and even, in some cases, to family or wedding-party members.

4. Your planner must be organized. It sounds like a no-brainer, but your planner must step up and have a fully detailed plan for your wedding. Paperwork and

contracts must all go through you. All decisions must be confirmed with you. You should be able to see your budget at all times. Your planner should never be late for meetings. You have to trust your planner to stay on top of all the little details.

5. Your planner should be creative and resourceful, combining your ideas with his or her own to create a cohesive theme. Planners should have books, magazines, blog links, and Pinterest boards to show you. They should provide you with color palates and design options.

✔ How to Let Friends Help If They Offer

Your friends are guests at your wedding. Guests! They should be treated as such. They will probably be giving you a gift. They'll probably be giving you emotional support through your stressful months of planning! No matter how bridezilla you get, no matter how crafty and do-it-yourself you are, and no matter how low your budget, your friends should not be working at your wedding. Respect those relationships — that means, don't ask them to move chairs, do postwedding cleanup or breakdown, provide food or bar service, be your pseudo-professional "official" photographer, help gather groups for formal photos, or be your DJ.

The following list is a great guidline for how to utilize the assistance of your friends:

- to officiate your wedding ceremony

- to sing or perform music at your wedding ceremony

- to make announcements (as long as there aren't too many of them, and as long as only one friend is in charge)

- to make your wedding cake (prior to the wedding day)

- to drop off setup and décor materials and to provide some setup assistance (only if you don't have a wedding planner, and only if those friends are not in the wedding party)

- to informally videotape the event (only if you have a friend who really enjoys being behind the camera — we all have one of those).

Remember, in most cases, your friends aren't professionals. If the video or the cake, for example, doesn't come out perfectly, you can't resent them for it. If they are in charge of wedding setup and they oversleep, have a family emergency, or a flat tire, you can't blame them — you're not paying them!

Chapter 4
Eleven Months Out

Create your guest list
Decide on your overall vision for the wedding
Line up locations
Visit venues
Using a private residence
Outdoor weddings
Restaurant weddings
Set your wedding date
Choose your wedding theme

✔ Create Your Guest List

Once you've selected your top three dates and set a budget, you can begin to think about whom to invite.

Wedding drama is certainly inevitable. We must accept that as fact. Family issues, budget stress, decision-making challenges . . . nothing seems to cause more anxiety than whom to invite, and perhaps more importantly, whom not to invite.

Creating a guest list should be one of the first things you do once you're ready to plan your wedding. I tell my clients to invite only people who will be thrilled to support them. In some cases, especially with family, this is easier said than done. As a wedding

planner, I've seen brides who were torn up because one of their aunts had signed an anti-same-sex marriage petition. (Her name was found on KnowThyNeighbor.blogs.com, a Web site that provides this information.) The aunt was invited anyway. I am hopeful that witnessing that beautiful wedding changed her heart and mind (as it often does). The reality is that not everyone in the world is happy about your lesbian wedding.

It's difficult knowing where to draw the line with your wedding-guest list, but you have to. Not only will the number of guests have budget implications, but it will have an impact on your options when it's time to go venue shopping!

Many couples find themselves having to invite friends or co-workers of their parents that they don't know very well (if at all). My best piece of advice is to create guest-list policies and be consistent with them. Start by asking yourselves the following questions — I call them "policy decisions":

- Work backward from your budget. If at least half of your budget will go toward food and beverages, how many people can you afford to host?

- Are ex-boyfriends and ex-girlfriends invited? We lesbians tend to love to keep in touch with our exes!

- Do you invite friends you haven't talked to in three or more years if the friendship has grown apart?

- Do you have to invite everyone whose weddings you've attended, even if the event was many years ago and the friendship hasn't survived?

- Do your work colleagues get invited?

- What about friends from high school and college that you've reconnected with via Facebook or another social networking site?

- Do you invite children? Do you let babies come?

- Do you allow your single friends to bring a plus-one? What if they are in a serious relationship but not living together? What if they are in a serious relationship and living together? What if they seem to have no hope of being in a serious relationship anytime soon?

- Are friends and neighbors of your parents invited? Your parents may want to honor some of their dearest friends with an invitation — but then again, some parents don't want to draw attention to their child's lesbian wedding.

- Are your parents' work colleagues invited?

A couple of etiquette notes: If someone is invited to your shower, he or she has to be invited to your wedding. This rule applies no matter who hosts the shower — family, attendants, or friends. If your work colleagues also throw you a shower, that doesn't mean they need a wedding invitation. Thank them at the event and immediately send them thank-you notes, too.

✔ Decide on Your Overall Vision for the Wedding

What kind of wedding do you want to have? Isn't that the million-dollar question? Most of us have been to many straight weddings before the laws began to change and allowed us to have our own lesbian weddings. So, now that you can have your own wedding, what kind do you want it to be? There are lots of choices. When I meet with clients, once I've established their projected guest count and budget, I usually start thinking about their wedding by breaking it down like a game. As a couple answers my questions, my mind narrows down the options as if the event were a Choose Your Own Adventure book. Once the questions are answered, I always have a short list of venues in my head. To start creating the type of wedding you want, here are some questions that you and your partner should be asking yourselves:

- Do you want a Saturday-night-dance-party type of event or a Sunday, elegant-brunch type of event? A daytime or a nighttime wedding?

- Do you want to have the ceremony in the same location as the reception?

- Are you planning to have a typical wedding with a ceremony, cocktail hour, dinner, and dancing? Or do you want a smaller wedding that more resembles a beautiful dinner party than a typical wedding? Or would you prefer a wedding that more resembles a cocktail party than a typical wedding?

- Do you want to have access to an outdoor area?

- Do you have a lot of friends and family traveling from out of state?

- Do you have a lot of big partiers/drinkers on your guest list?

- Is your style (a) urban/contemporary, (b) industrial/loft-like, (c) country/rustic, (d) historic/classically elegant, (e) casual/beachy?

- Do you require a view of some sort?

- Are you planning to feed everyone a full meal, or would you rather have a cocktail-party-type atmosphere the whole time?

Asking yourselves these questions will quickly narrow the list of potential sites. As a wedding planner, it's my job to ask questions like this when I first meet a couple. You

can have the world's largest Pinterest board, but you're ultimately going to want a wedding that reflects your personality and your culture, your sense of humor, and your sense of style — not someone else's.

✔ Line Up Locations

When you start doing your venue shopping, be sure to look at the following categories as possible host sites. You may be able to cross some of these types of spaces off the list right away, or there may be a particular type of space that you're immediately drawn to:

- halls (including Elks Lodge, Knights of Columbus, and the like)

- hotels, resorts, and inns (the Kimpton chain is the most LGBT-friendly of the lot)

- historic spaces (including old mansions, municipal buildings, libraries, and historic homes)

- museums (art museums and museums of industry, technology, science, and so forth)

- colleges and universities

- private clubs (country clubs, golf clubs, yacht clubs, and other social, members-only clubs)

- restaurants

- function spaces (a catch-all that may include conference centers, retreats, banquet halls, lofts, wineries, and other venues)

Narrowing down the categories to the one you want is the first step in the venue selection process. The right site can reflect your wedding vision without necessarily needing a great deal of décor. In most cases, when you book a venue, you'll receive the space for eight hours, which means a five-hour wedding. That leaves three additional hours — two for setup and one for breakdown — which is the industry

standard. If your ceremony is in the same place as the reception, that usually cuts into the five-hour rental time unless you pay for an additional 30- to 60-minute rental.

Please plan accordingly when you think through your wedding-decoration and setup projects. You have a limited time in which to work, and some venues won't let you drop off items prior to your wedding day.

✔ Visit Venues

One of the first steps in the planning process (after you set your budget and guest list) is to go venue shopping. I highly recommend you start your search, even though you may not yet have a wedding date in mind. Finding a place to get married is one of the most stressful parts of planning — it's such a big deal, really — especially if the venue also provides the food and drink. In many areas, there are tons of choices, which can make coming up with a short list fairly overwhelming.

When you go venue shopping, I highly recommend that you check out about five to six places in one day. I call these marathon site-visits. Each venue will be fresh in your mind as you compare them, and the cream of the crop will stick out in your mind. As you're shopping, find out the answers to the following questions, especially if you are having a wedding with an onsite ceremony, cocktail hour, dinner, and dancing:

• If applicable, have any same-sex weddings been performed at the site?

• Is there a policy of acceptance throughout their entire staff, not just the member of the sales team who wants you to book the venue, but also the waitstaff who will be serving you your dinner? (This is especially important for a transgender bride or groom.)

• If applicable, how many overnight guest rooms are available for guests? Are there any minimum-nights'-stay requirements? Is a discount available on large blocks of rooms?

- Ensure there are two-plus rooms/spaces you'll have access to or, if it's one large room, that it can be partitioned or screened. One space will be for the ceremony/dinner and the second for the cocktail hour.

- Is there plenty of space inside for a ceremony, if the weather is poor, that can then be turned over for a reception while the guests go somewhere else during cocktail hour?

- Where will the cocktail hour be held?

- Is there space for a band or DJ? Are there plenty of electrical outlets? Are there any noise restrictions or ordinances?

- What is the fee for the space? Is the fee waived with a food and beverage minimum? Is the fee waived with guest room bookings?

- Is there an additional fee for an onsite ceremony? If so, does that extra fee get you an extra hour of rental time (six hours instead of five), or does an onsite ceremony cut into your five-hour rental time?

- Is there a "holding area" where you can get ready before the ceremony, or wait before the processional?

- What other fees are there? Do they charge for bartenders and cake cutting? What about security?

- Do they add gratuity and administrative charges to the bill?

- Can all of your guests fit into one function room, or do you have to use adjoining side rooms?

- Does the venue provide tables and chairs, or do they need to be rented? What size tables and what kinds of chairs do they own?

- Does the venue provide a dance floor, or does that need to be rented?

- Does the venue have liability insurance? Do they require that vendors carry it also?

- What do their chairs, flatware, glassware, china, and linens look like? Do their house linens drape all the way to the floor? (You don't want to see the legs of the tables.)

• How much time prior to and after the wedding is available for setup and breakdown? Does the venue staff help with that? What services does their wedding or event coordinator provide? Does he or she help with setting up all of your personal details or touches? Will that person confirm your other vendors and send them a schedule? Will he or she line up the wedding party and send you down the aisle? *Note:* Most venues don't provide these services, but if they do, you may be able to avoid hiring a day-of coordinator.

• Is there a sound system that an iPod or CD player can be plugged into?

Green Tip: There are many hotels and other venues that are energy efficient, use environmentally friendly products, have comprehensive recycling programs, and minimize water, waste, and toxins. Other spaces charge a rental fee that supports efforts to preserve beautiful places. When you're looking to be green, consider these spaces first!

Once you choose a venue, you'll be working closely with them throughout the process. It's very important for you to feel comfortable with the place you choose, especially if they are also providing food and beverages. They will be receiving the bulk of your wedding budget, so you'll want to be happy about your choice!

✔ Using a Private Residence

In theory, there are some advantages to planning a wedding at your home or another private residence. The home could have a special meaning to you. You could save on a venue rental fee. You are not limited by an eight-hour rental period and can set up and break down at your leisure. The party could go all night if you want.

But don't be blinded by the advantages. Think through these potential obstacles before making your final decision:

- How is the septic system? Can it handle 50 or more guests? Are there two or more restrooms that guests can use? Will you have to rent portapotties or a luxury portapotty trailer?

- How is the parking situation? Is there enough parking for all of the vendors in the driveway? What will you do about parking for guests? Will you have to hire a valet or rent a lot and provide shuttle service?

- Is the home big enough for everyone to be inside for dinner and dancing? Or will you need to rent a tent to accommodate everyone? Are you prepared to deal with the damage that tents (and the tent delivery truck) may cause to the lawn?

- Is there a good spot on the property for a wedding ceremony? What if it rains?

- Are there any noise ordinances in the city or town where the wedding would be held?

- Is there a large kitchen onsite? The caterer will have a lot of food to warm up or prepare and will need plenty of counter space and ovens. If you can't offer that, the caterer may have to set up a catering tent, or you may have to rent convection ovens.

- How many amps of electricity does the home have? Are there some circuits with available power? If you are bringing in a tent, the lighting and heating of it will require significant power. If you are bringing in a DJ or band, they'll need substantial power as well. As will the portapotty. Find out if you have enough electrical power to support the event or whether you'll need to rent a generator.

In general, unless it's a very well-equipped property or you're considering inviting fewer than 50 guests, I advise against holding a wedding in someone's home or on their property. The logistics can get very complicated, and if you decide to go this route, I would definitely suggest that you hire a wedding planner to make sure that all of these details are covered.

Please use a caterer for your wedding in a private residence. Don't rely on your friends, family, or yourself to prepare food. If you need to, you can prepare the food in advance and rent waitstaff and bartenders to serve it, but please outsource at least some of this for your own sanity!

✔ Outdoor Weddings

Now, I know that I live and work mostly in the Northeast, so I have a bias. We don't have sunshine every day like they do in Los Angeles, so we always, always, always have to have a rain plan for weddings. We have our beautiful coastline and many people love beachy weddings, but there has to be a rain plan, and unfortunately sometimes that rain plan doesn't have the same appeal as the outdoor affair.

If you find yourself in a situation where your perfectly planned outdoor wedding gets rained out and you're forced inside, think about asking your photographer to do another shoot of you and your partner (kind of like an engagement shoot) in your wedding wardrobe on another day when it's beautiful outside.

Other important considerations when planning an outdoor wedding:

- Is a tent required, or is there enough room inside if the weather is poor?

- How cold does the area get in the evening? Will heaters be required inside the tent?

- How warm does the area get in the evening? Will air conditioners or fans be required inside the tent?

- Do the grounds get buggy during certain seasons?

- Are there any drainage issues that could make for excess mud?

- How far do the guests have to walk to get to the restrooms?

- Is there plenty of space inside for a ceremony if the weather is poor, and can it then be turned over for a reception while the guests go somewhere else during cocktail hour?

- Is there adequate lighting on the property in the evening?

- Are there any eyesores that may need to be covered up or screened off?

- Is there any foot traffic that may pass through the area, or is there security to ensure that your space is completely private?

TENTS AND DANCE FLOORS

If you do have to rent a tent, you should book one as soon as you find the venue. Keep in mind that you'll also have to rent a dance floor. Tents come in all shapes and sizes. The tent rental company will be able to give you suggestions on the right size and type of tent for your wedding, based on your unique specifications. You will also have to rent lights for inside the tent. The tent company should provide you with some options, which may include lanterns, paper lanterns, small white bulbs around the perimeter, larger white bulbs around the perimeter, or more. The tent company will also offer heaters and air conditioners, which may be necessary depending on where you live.

✔ Restaurant Weddings

Restaurants make a great option, especially for smaller weddings. If it's a restaurant you already love, you know that the food is going to be great. You probably already like the décor and may not need to spruce it up a lot. You may even know the owners. Consider these factors when deciding whether a restaurant wedding is right for you:

If your wedding is large enough, you may have to do a full buyout, which means that the restaurant will close to the public and you'll have to guarantee spending as much as the restaurant typically makes on that given night. In some cases, this can be as little as $5000 or $10,000 or as much as $40,000.

If your wedding is small, you may be in the restaurant's private dining room, which typically has a room fee and/or a minimum food and beverage cost. The room may not be big enough for anything other than dinner.

Are you hoping to have a full ceremony, cocktail hour, dinner, and dancing? If so, then is there a space in the restaurant to accommodate all of that? Most restaurants do not have a good onsite ceremony option, and cocktail hour may have to be forced around the dinner tables. That's not ideal because then the dinner tables get messed up and guests start to sit down early.

Is there room for a dance floor already? Or do you have to break down dinner tables to create one? Breaking down a few dinner tables is a pretty quick process, but just consider this when choosing your space.

All things considered, though, if you have the option of using a great restaurant that has grounds that are big enough for an outdoor ceremony and cocktail hour, you may find this to be a fantastic value for your wedding.

✔ Set Your Wedding Date

How do you figure out when to get married? I always encourage couples to have an open mind about their wedding date.

Blackout dates. Start with a specific month or two, and ask your closest guests to tell you any blackout dates within that time frame. For example, a mom of a bride may already be booked to attend a major work conference. Once you've eliminated blackout dates, rank your top three available dates. Use this when venue shopping, so you can have the greatest number of options. I'd hate for you to not be able to marry in your dream venue because it's already booked. Flexibility in your wedding date can help avoid that problem.

Travel arrangements. Choose a date that gives your guests at least six months to make travel arrangements, if necessary. They may have to arrange for child care as well as to take time off from work. Those coming in from other places will need time to get the best airfare.

Weather concerns. Keep in mind any climate or seasonal factors that may affect your wedding plans. For example, if you are dreaming of an outdoor wedding, do some research on the months with the lowest amount of precipitation. Obviously, if you live in a hurricane zone, you will want to consider a date outside of hurricane season.

Holiday weekends. Holiday weekends have pros and cons for weddings. They give you the option of having a Saturday or Sunday wedding but may bring with them a premium for airfare, hotels, and/or paying for child and pet care. Major holidays (such as Thanksgiving and Christmas) may bring with them premium charges from vendors who aren't able to spend that time with their own families.

Avoiding prime dates. Keep in mind that an off-season Friday or Sunday date can give you leverage in negotiating discounts with vendors.

Bottom line: Although your own wishes are important, please keep your guests in mind as well when choosing a date.

Day or Evening?

Do you want an evening affair, or are you thinking of a daytime wedding? There are pros and cons to both evening and daytime celebrations. The overall guest experience will vary depending on the time of day. Be aware that guests are more inclined to dance at night, if you are imagining a lot of dancing at your wedding.

The time of day of your event can have a significant impact on your food budget. Guests generally drink less at daytime events. If you're having a daytime wedding, you can serve brunch-type food. (Think how cheap eggs are!)

✔ Choose Your Wedding Theme

Weddings are a great way to express your design philosophy! But what *is* your design philosophy? Look around your home and in your closet. Think about your cultural background. Since your wedding is all about celebrating you and your fiancée, then I urge you to have fun with a color or design theme.

I suggest that each couple have two to four wedding colors, with one as the primary color and two or three as accent colors. These colors can be carried throughout your wedding, beginning with the save-the-date card and all the way through to the wedding cake, table linens, flowers, and so on.

For clients who are struggling to decide what colors to use, wedding planners often help them create an inspiration board, which you can do yourself on Pinterest.com. Pinterest is basically a way to "clip" digital images and "pin" them to a themed board. You may have one board of invitation inspiration, another of food inspiration, another of décor, etc.

Inspiration boards and Pinterest boards are essentially a collage of things that you like: they could be colors, objects, and/or themes. The images could come from weddings, from magazines or books, or from nature. The possibilities are limitless!

Chapter 5
Ten Months Out

Choose your officiant
Book hotel rooms for out-of-town guests
Send out save-the-date cards
Establish your budget priorities

✔ Choose Your Officiant

If you ask me, the most important part of a wedding is the "I dos." They are, after all, what the whole day is about. A marriage is a big deal, or it should be. With same-sex marriages becoming legal in more states, I am a big fan of meaningful and personal wedding ceremonies.

You've probably been to at least one wedding with a snooze-worthy officiant, and you've probably heard the same boring homily or speech over and over again. When hiring an officiant, make sure he or she has experience with same-sex couples or is comfortable with your marriage, and will be able to contribute to the spirit and joy of your ceremony. Don't be afraid to check references or ask for audio or video recordings of a ceremony officiated by him or her.

Let's talk about your options:

Guest Officiant

Many states will authorize a specific person to perform marriages on a specific date. There is typically a nominal fee and some light paperwork required for the privilege. It often takes 60 or more days to process the application.

In many states, a loved one can get a "day pass" to officiate your wedding ceremony. There's some paperwork and a fee, but it is perfectly legal and is a great way to personalize your wedding. If you are marrying in a state where a "day pass" is not permitted (such as New York), it's still quite easy for someone to get ordained online. Just Google "online ordination" and some options will appear. That person may then have to register with the clerk of the city or town where the marriage is being performed.

One of my favorite wedding ceremonies was officiated by an out-of-state friend of the couple. She came very prepared and worked with me to make sure the rehearsal and ceremony went smoothly. She was clear, articulate, humorous, and perfectly reverent.

Justice of the Peace

A justice of the peace (a JP) is an officer of the state legally allowed to officiate weddings in some — but not all — states. The rules vary from state to state, but in those that have a policy against discrimination on the basis of sexual orientation, a JP may not legally discriminate against you. (Nonetheless, a JP may try to avoid performing your ceremony by saying, for example, that he or she is booked for your requested date.) Many JPs have sample ceremonies and vows that they present as options to a couple. Some JPs will offer a custom ceremony-writing option, while others will not. Usually, JPs do not attend the wedding rehearsal. The average fee charged by a justice of the peace for a basic, noncustom ceremony without rehearsal is from $100 to $200.

Judge

In some states, judges are authorized to officiate marriages; in other states they're not. As with JPs, some judges will provide a couple with sample ceremonies and vows, and some will prepare a customized ceremony. Many judges will not rehearse the ceremony with the couple.

City Clerk

A city or county clerk is authorized to marry individuals. These weddings are usually quick, held in the clerk's office, and as a rule, the clerk will not have met the couple before the ceremony. In these cases, there is no custom-written ceremony, no rehearsal, and nothing religious about the ceremony.

Celebrant

You might want to hire a trained celebrant to perform your ceremony. Celebrants USA is an institute that intensely trains individuals to write and create meaningful and personal ceremonies for weddings and other major life events. Graduates are authorized to officiate marriage ceremonies, and these ceremonies are custom written. Celebrants attend and run the wedding rehearsal and may or may not use religious traditions, depending on your preference. Technically, they are authorized to officiate weddings as members of the clergy, but that doesn't mean the wedding has to be religious — unless you want it to be. My own wedding was officiated by a celebrant (Cindy Matchett — we love her!) who later officiated our son's baby blessing.

Member of the Clergy

Clergy members include rabbis, priests, reverends, ministers, and others affiliated with a place of worship who are authorized to officiate weddings. Ceremonies performed by clergy members will most certainly have a religious slant, regardless of whether or not they're held in a place of worship. In many cases, the clergy member requires the couple to undergo prewedding counseling, and sometimes he or she will require the couple to join the church or synagogue if they are not already members. In chapter 9, I'll explain some of the faiths that allow their clergy to officiate same-sex marriage ceremonies.

It's traditional for the officiant and his or her spouse (if applicable) to be invited to the rehearsal dinner and wedding. The officiants I know usually decline because they have their own family obligations and perform at many weddings. But it is a nice gesture to invite them nonetheless.

✔ Book Hotel Rooms for Out-of-Town Guests

I plan a lot of destination weddings that involve guests' traveling to a place where same-sex marriage is legal. I encourage couples to book rooms in a hotel that's close to interesting restaurants or tourist hot spots, so your guests have activities to enjoy either before or after your big event. Keep in mind that they will only be at your wedding for five or six hours, but they may be in the city or town for a full weekend. Typically, a hotel offers some kind of discount for your guests when you book a block of more than five rooms a night.

If you can set up transportation from the hotel to the wedding location and back, that's even better for your guests, who won't have to worry about drinking and driving.

✔ Send Out Save-the-Date Cards

Once you have your venue chosen, date set, and guest hotel booked, get busy on the save-the-date notices.

At this point, you may have determined a theme for your wedding, and the notices can be the first item that reflects your thematic decision. Keep an eye on the big picture as you create these cards. If at all possible, indicate the URL of your wedding Web site right on the card.

SAVE THE DATE!
— Saturday, May 18, 2013 —
for the wedding of
Deidre Maria Dixon
and
Monica Anne Golding
OAKVILLE, ONTARIO
— *Formal invitation to follow.* —
WWW.DEIDREANDMONICA.OURWEDDING.COM

The save-the-dates are the first correspondence most people will have from you about your wedding. You can send these out up to a year in advance. This way your guests can make their own travel plans (if applicable) and make arrangements to take off from work, if they need to.

While it's nice to have the save-the-date be part of the cohesive stationery design, you can be completely whimsical if you prefer. I had a couple choose a save-the-date that looked like a flyer for a country music show because they met in Nashville. I had others choose a vintage postcard style.

One of the big questions I get is whether save-the-dates can be e-mailed to guests, rather than put in the mail. Sure. If most of your guests are online, then absolutely send e-mail save-the-dates through PaperlessPost.com or similar sites. Just don't expect to get away with that for the actual wedding invitations. Paper invitations are here to stay!

✔ Establish Your Budget Priorities

The economy is hitting everyone hard. A tight budget doesn't mean that your wedding design needs to be seriously compromised — you can still plan a stunning wedding. One trend we've noticed is that couples are still planning spectacular weddings, but they are inviting fewer people. Since food and beverages are typically the mostly costly elements of a wedding, a smaller party can mean significant savings. To help you establish your budget priorities, I'm including a number of cost-saving tips in this section. It may be very important to you to have an amazing venue that costs thousands of dollars to rent, but you might not care about letterpress wedding invitations. You may want the best band in the world and not really mind having a wedding on a Friday in February. I've noticed that my clients, in general, focus on the venue, the food, and the entertainment, with everything else a lower priority.

CONSIDER THESE COST-SAVING TIPS:

• Plan a winter wedding or a wedding on a Friday night or a Sunday brunch— you may get vendor discounts (you should definitely ask!), and food and beverage minimums may be lower. Avoid high-demand dates such as Valentine's Day and New Year's Eve. Consider having an afternoon event, at which alcoholic beverage consumption will be significantly lower than at an evening event.

• Have your wedding in a restaurant or a venue where there's no fee to rent the space.

• If you are wearing one, choose a wedding dress from a selection of bridesmaid dresses, not from the typical wedding gown department.

• Skip some of the stationery elements that are costly and environmentally wasteful. This means: no favors (which are often left behind), no ceremony programs, and perhaps a seating chart instead of escort cards. You can even skip save-the-date cards.

• If you have guests who love to drink, consider an open bar with only wine and beer, plus perhaps one delicious signature cocktail.

• Consider putting a time limit on the hosted portion of the beverage service. Close the bar 30 to 45 minutes before the end of the event and then serve only soft drinks and coffee.

• If you are hosting a full bar, consider limiting the grade of liquor. Hosting a midgrade liquor selection rather than a combination of mid- and premium-grade liquors can trim 10 to 15 percent off your bar bill.

• Have your ceremony and reception in the same venue. Many places will not charge a ceremony fee (like a house of worship would), and you can save on the cost of limos. Our wedding venue was a block away from our hotel, so the hotel guests and brides arrived on foot.

• Choose flowers that are in season when considering your wedding colors and floral designs. In-season flowers are much less expensive (and don't have the negative environmental impact of those transported from around the world). We used hydrangea and peonies as the primary flowers for our early July wedding.

- Use lots and lots and lots of candles!

- Cupcakes are cute and quite inexpensive, sometimes as little as $1.50 each, instead of the $3.50 per slice that's the standard minimum for wedding cakes. Still want a cake cutting? Order a small nine-inch cake to cut!

- If you have an amazingly articulate, eloquent friend or family member whom you would trust to officiate your wedding ceremony, he or she can do so for $50 with a permit from the state. Contrast this cost with the fee of justices of the peace, who charge $150 and up, and those of rabbis, ministers, and celebrants who often charge $500 or more.

- Have a family or friend do your hair and makeup.

- True do-it-yourselfers (DIYers) can save money with homemade centerpieces, handcrafted invitations, and countless other fun DIY projects.

- Go to Etsy.com and find small creative businesses that will custom-make everything for you, from wedding dresses to invitations.

- Finally, if you're really stressed about money, elope! If that's not an option, hiring a wedding planner can save you 10 to 20 percent on services like catering, photography, floral design, and more.

Chapter 6
Nine Months Out

Set up your wedding registry
Choose your photographer

✔ Set Up Your Wedding Registry

Are you registering for gifts? It seems like the answer should be obvious, but in fact, many lesbian couples do not. The top two reasons for not registering that I've observed are:

- Many lesbian couples have already been together for years, accumulating a houseful of great stuff — and just don't need to register.

- Many lesbian couples would rather have their guests support an important charity instead of spending money on gifts.

However, many more couples *do* register for gifts, assuming that, since people are going to give them stuff anyway, it might as well be stuff they actually want. Be aware, however, that while most guests give a gift to the couple, they are not obligated to do so, and you should never expect one.

You should note that most stores are still very heterosexist when it comes to wedding registries. There's a good chance you'll see "bride's name" and "groom's name" on paperwork and on Web sites. There may be assumptions made about your relationship if you go to the store in person to register for items. The salesclerk might not be enthusiastic. The good news is that the most popular stores allow you to set up your registry online if you would prefer to do so.

So, How Do You Appropriately Create a Registry?

As a couple, make a list of what you need to furnish and decorate your home. Plan out décor and colors. What is your style: contemporary, traditional, country, or something else?

- Register for more items than you actually need. Guests like choices, and you're not going to get everything on your list. Put yourself in your guests' situation: if all that's left on the registry is an iron and a spatula set, they won't have any fun shopping for you.

- Register for gifts across a spectrum of budgets, so your guests have options depending on what they can afford. (Don't make assumptions about people's generosity — or lack thereof. You'll be surprised by who gives what!) This is also important because, if you do have a wedding shower, you'll likely get lower-priced gifts at that event and more generous gifts for your wedding.

- Remember that it is never good etiquette to include registry information with your wedding invitations. However, you may include it on shower invitations, or you may post links to the registries on your wedding Web site. Be sure to include the wedding Web site URL on the logistics card that's enclosed with your invitation suite.

- Provide the store with an address where gifts can be sent. Your guests will like having the option of not bringing the physical gifts to the wedding.

- Consider registering through a charity like the Human Rights Campaign (HRC) or Marriage Equality USA, both of which allow you to set up an online registry page. Guests can make a donation in your name and feel good about their choice.

• Yes, you *can* register for a honeymoon if you wish. Some honeymoon registries double as travel agents, so you can book your plans directly through them. Others, like Honeyfund, are merely vessels by which you receive checks from your guests. You can indicate where you are going and outline what you may do while you are there. Guests may, for example, treat you to a spa visit, a sailing expedition, dinner on the beach, or a guided tour through a rainforest. It's a win-win for you and your guests.

✔ Choose Your Photographer

Wedding photography is an investment. Don't skimp on it! Your photos are one of the few things that will remain long after your wedding is over. You probably already know that most wedding photographers shoot with digital cameras rather than film, but if you have a preference you'll want to address it with the photographers you interview. Here are some other questions to ask yourselves before you begin to call photographers:

Are you planning to see each other before the wedding? This traditional custom doesn't have to be observed. Most lesbian couples I've worked with have had their formal group photos taken before the ceremony so that they can immediately enjoy cocktail hour with their guests. (As a point of reference, many straight couples first see each other when the bride walks down the aisle and have their formal photos taken during cocktail hour.)

Do you want a photographer who will shoot all day? You might like to have the photographer take shots of you and your fiancée getting ready for the wedding and, as mentioned above, take formal photos before the ceremony. On the other hand, perhaps you'd be happy with coverage of just the ceremony and reception.

What photographic style are you drawn to? Do you prefer photos that look like fine art or that capture little moments? Do you like photos that look like they could be from a fashion magazine? Think about the kind you like best.

Are you planning to walk down two aisles or enter your wedding ceremony from two different directions? If so, you may want to consider asking the photographer to bring an assistant who can shoot down the second aisle.

Will you want a wedding album? Wedding albums are provided by most photographers (as an additional service), but you can also create your own beautiful, archival-quality album through a Web site like AlbumBoutique.com.

Once you've answered the above questions, you'll be much better prepared to meet a photographer. It's important to choose someone with whom you feel there's a good chemistry. If your personalities match, there are some requisite questions to ask during the interview, in addition to reviewing his or her portfolio:

- Have you photographed a same-sex wedding before?

- How would you describe your style?

- How many photos do you shoot at a typical wedding?

- Do we get proofs of the images?

- What level of editing do you provide photos before we receive them? Do you do color correction, crop out EXIT signs, and the like?

- Do we get full use of high-resolution images after the wedding?

- Do we book an album through you, or can we make our own?

- How long does it take for you to give us the high-resolution wedding photos?

- What is your backup plan in case of emergency?

- How long does it take for you to produce an album?

- Do you offer an assistant/second shooter and, if so, at what price?

- Do you offer an engagement photo shoot and, if so, for what price?

- How is your pricing structured?

Chapter 7
Eight Months Out

Decide whether you want a DJ or a band
Book the emcee
Consider an iPod reception
Look for other entertainment
Hire a videographer

✔ Decide Whether You Want a DJ or a Band

Music is obviously a critical element to your wedding. You're going to have to figure out whether you prefer a DJ or a band, and which you can afford. Lots of couples have a bias against DJs, expecting that they'll be big on self-promotion and play line dances — in fact, 95 percent of my clients explicitly say, "I don't want to hear 'The Chicken Dance' at my wedding." Who can blame them?

A band can really get the guests up and moving on the dance floor, and that kind of energy can be infectious, but band members have to eat dinner, too, and sometimes the whole crew will disappear without putting on a CD for dinner music. And then all you hear is the scraping of your guests' forks on plates. Not cool.

Let's go through some pros and cons of a DJ versus a band:

- The DJ can obtain and play virtually any song you want to hear at your wedding. The band will have a limited repertoire and will usually only be willing to learn one or two songs for your wedding. Bands often lack skills in certain genres (for example, if hip-hop's your thing, will your band be able to accommodate your taste?).

- Many DJs have a reputation for being cheesy. Many will bring props, such as inflatable instruments, cowboy hats, and boas. They have been known to hang tacky promotional signage, talk too much, and seek to be the center of attention. Bands seldom exhibit such inappropriate wedding behavior.

- The DJ will cost somewhere between $500 and $2500 (on average), whereas bands typically start at $3500 and go up from there.

- Bands have been known to take long dinner breaks without providing backup music.

- The energy created by a DJ will be limited to the music he or she plays, whereas there's something powerful about the presence of a live band whose music can get your guests up and dancing.

- Both DJs and bands can provide music for the ceremony and cocktail hour. In most cases, you will be charged extra for this service. Typically, only a few band members will perform during the ceremony and cocktail hour, with the rest arriving for the reception.

- It's nice to have live music for the ceremony and cocktail hour — but a string or jazz trio or quartet could run you upwards of $2000 more than the cost of a DJ.

- Having a band is like being at a live concert. It's a real treat for your guests and tends to be more memorable than a DJ. For extra large weddings, a band makes a bigger impact than a DJ. At a recent wedding I planned, we booked both a band and a DJ. When the band took a break, the DJ took over. There was never a lull in the music and the energy stayed up all night. It was the best-case scenario.

✔ Book the Emcee

Whether you choose a DJ or a band, be sure that you're comfortable with the emcee. This individual is going to be managing the flow of your wedding. A good emcee is critical! Make sure the emcee is someone who will be unobtrusive and not talk too much, but who will be personable, professional, and clearly heard.

✔ Consider an iPod Reception

An increasing number of couples are creating iPod playlists for their wedding soundtrack. If done properly, this can be a major savings, though it may not be worth the hassle of setting it up right. Be sure that your venue has a sound system you can plug your iPod into. If there's no sound system, be prepared to rent one.

As you put together your playlist, make sure there are no gaps between songs. (Even a five-second gap can kill the momentum on the dance floor!) Create individual playlists for each stage of the wedding and identify them ("cocktail hour," "first dance," "cake cutting," etc.).

✔ Look for Other Entertainment

We had a surprise guest at our wedding, and she was fierce! Jen took the mic and introduced her after our strawberry-shortcake cutting. Her name is Mizery, and she's Boston's most legendary drag queen.

Jen felt strongly that we needed to give our wedding an extra bit of oomph to entertain our guests. Above all, she did not want a boring wedding. I was thinking we'd hire a fire dancer, but Jen often gets her way and is usually right, so we hired Mizery. Well, our wedding certainly wasn't boring, and as Jen promised, when Mizery appeared, the party really got started.

Mizery performed "We Are Family" and got some guests up and dancing with her — and then she did a split! You had to see it to believe it. The look on our guests' faces was priceless and people are still talking about it.

Mizery added a little bit of fabulousness to our wedding, but I've also had clients hire a fire dancer, tango dancers, flamenco performers, caricature artists, karaoke hosts, and the like. You get the drift . . . a little bit of entertainment (and I do mean a short piece) goes a long way toward creating wedding memories.

✔ Hire a Videographer

There are lots of ways to save money on your wedding. But do not skimp on a photographer and videographer.

Jen and I named photography and videography as priorities for our wedding. Wedding videography has long held the stereotype of being tacky, with a giant spotlight taking up too much room on the dance floor and annoying guests. We've all seen the handheld, shaky, horribly edited footage with cheesy glamour-shot type designs. But it would be unfair to paint all videographers with the same brush. There are some video artists who can truly capture your wedding memories forever. The best videographers in the industry are trying to escape the stereotype and prefer to be called "filmmakers." Like your photographs, a good wedding video is an investment, something you will treasure for years to come and share with your loved ones. I know that our child will one day love our wedding film.

Again, you spend a lot of time with the videographer, so you'll want to make sure you click! Here are questions and things to think about as you prepare for the interview process:

- Has the videographer worked with same-sex couples before or shot any same-sex weddings?

- What's the videographer's style?

- Ask to see an entire wedding video (not just a trailer) that the videographer has created. The trailer is just the highlights: be sure to see how the videographer covers an entire wedding.

- While watching the video, pay attention to the sound quality, especially during key moments. You'll want to remember the vows and toasts. Is the bestie's toast loud and clear? Can you hear the sweeties say "I do"?

- Ask the videographer whether his or her equipment is wireless. Does he or she have wireless mics? Does he or she have wireless lights?

- Speaking of lights, will a giant spotlight on the dance floor kill the mood? Or worse yet, a giant spotlight in your guests' eyes?

- How will the videographer capture the wedding music? Can he or she plug into a DJ or band mixing board?

- Does he or she shoot in high definition or standard definition?

- How many people on the videographer's crew will be filming the wedding?

- How long is the turnaround time for an average wedding-video edit?

- How long are the final edited videos?

- What kind of music is used in the final edited videos? Does it have to be selected from a certain royalty-free song list?

- How many DVDs do you receive as finished products?

- How do you order extra copies and for what cost?

- What is the business's emergency plan in the event of equipment failure or illness?

Chapter 8
Seven Months Out

Decide what you want to wear
Shop for the wedding gown or dress
Shop for the suit or tux
Make up your mind about hair and makeup

✔ Decide What You Want to Wear

Theoretically, it should be super fun to pick out what you'll wear to your lesbian wedding. That said, the outfit-selection process can be stressful. I try to guide my clients to make good choices that reflect their taste (without providing too much of my own opinion).

I talk with a lot of brides, and one of their biggest sources of angst and frustration is the issue of what to wear at their wedding. A lot of lesbian brides don't want to wear a wedding gown (and a lot of lesbian brides would rather be called bridegrooms). I didn't wear a wedding gown myself.

Sometimes you have to get really creative.

Many of my clients have chosen to wear custom creations or have bought off the rack at Banana Republic, J.Crew, Hugo Boss, Nordstrom, or Bloomingdale's. I've seen brides wear tunics, saris, white tea dresses, colored dresses, and of course traditional wedding gowns. Some have chosen black suits and tuxedoes, others preferred white, navy, or gray suits and tuxedoes. There's no tradition here: use your imagination and allow yourself to be inspired.

If you are interested in the trends, my survey of about 300 lesbian couples indicated the following stats about what they wore:

- 46% of lesbian couples had one partner in a wedding gown or dress and one in a pants suit or tuxedo

- 42% of lesbian couples had both partners in a wedding gown or dress

- 12% of lesbian couples had both partners in a pants suit or tuxedo

✔ Shop for the Wedding Gown or Dress

Many lesbian brides want to wear a beautiful, white wedding gown. They want the fantasy that they grew up with, the feeling, as one of my brides put it, "of being in a big room full of wedding dresses, surrounded by my friends and a bottle of Champagne." Their wedding day is the day that they get to live the fairytale, be the princess.

If you are such a bride, as my wife Jen was, there's a good chance you're going to be asked questions about your groom when you go dress shopping. My best advice: when you call to make an appointment, explicitly tell the person at the store that yours is a lesbian wedding and that there is no groom. State that you want to be clear about this from the beginning so there's no confusion.

> **TRANSGENDER TIP:** It will be especially important to come out over the phone and again before your appointment begins.

Gown or dress shopping is a very emotional process. And it's one that you should start fairly early on in your planning process. In a way, getting a dress symbolizes that the wedding is actually happening. So, how do you choose a dress that makes you feel confident, sexy, and comfortable? How do you pick out the one garment that will reflect your personality on the biggest day of your life? Start by asking, what looks good on your body? Be honest with yourself. Are you petite or tall? What are your best features and what are your problem areas? Are you curvy or tall and narrow? There's truly a dress for everyone. In general, empire, A-line, and ball gowns are the most "forgiving" dress styles for those of us with a little extra.

Bustles and Alterations

When you go shopping, there's a good chance that your size may not be in stock. Wedding-dress vendors typically carry a few sample sizes (around size 8–10) in each style and then clamp the back so you get a sense of how the dress will actually look. After that, they'll take your measurements, and those will be used to create your made-to-order dress. After the dress comes in (it may take from four to six months), alterations may still be needed (running several hundred dollars and up), so be sure to plan accordingly.

I've noticed that most of my lesbian brides who wear dresses forgo a train on the dress. If you do have a train, a bustle will have to be added by a seamstress, so that your dress can be bustled for the reception. At the fitting where the seamstress is pinning the bustle, make sure it's high enough so you can dance at the reception! This may mean busting out a few dance moves during the fitting!

If you have a bustle, be sure to put someone (your wedding planner or your best person) in charge of learning how to tie the bustle on your wedding day! Some bustles are snapped or hooked, but most commonly they're tied with a series of ribbons. Bustles do break, so be sure to include heavy-duty safety pins (diaper pins work well) in your wedding-day emergency kit (just in case!).

✔ Shop for the Suit or Tux

Lesbian brides who do not want to wear wedding gowns have a harder time. The options are just so limited. Here are some of the challenges you'll encounter if you are looking for a suit or tux in a store:

- If you want to wear a white suit and your wedding is in the summer, you will have a tough time shopping for it before spring. And you might not find something right away, which brings an extra layer of wedding stress. Conversely, winter-weight white suits are scarce in the summer.

- If you want to wear a suit and not look like you're in something you can hang

he closet and wear to work on Monday (that is, something that is not
the-office looking), your options will be further limited. Suits with
ape to the design can be scarce!

ok for a men's tuxedo to rent or buy, there's a very good chance that
the fit won't be right. The legs and sleeves will probably be too long and the
shoulders too broad. If you have a bust, the jacket probably leaves no room for
that. You're going to have to find an LGBT-friendly tailor who will alter the
heck out of that suit — but it can be done.

> **TRANSGENDER TIP:** Depending on your body type, you may have to have a suit
> custom made by a tailor, or the suit you buy may need to be significantly
> altered for you.

Truly, your best bet is to approach your wedding suit the same way a woman wearing
a wedding gown might approach her attire: see it as an investment. Your suit doesn't
have to be something you'll wear again. It's special, and it's okay if it stays in the
back of your closet for eternity. If you truly want to look your sharpest, I strongly
recommend that you have a suit custom made by a tailor, which can run $1000 and
up. It's a lot of money, but it's worth it. The suit will be made with the finest fabrics,
and perfectly cut for your body. You will look your best. I highly recommend that

you seek the services of an expert tailor in your area. If
budget constraints prevent you from going this route,
don't worry — you have another option . . .

Fourteen

Because I saw that it was a giant problem to find
attractive wedding suits over the years, I was committed
to finding a solution. When I met fashion designer
Marialexandra Garcia, a partnership was born. We
created a line of ready-to-wear suits, tuxes, and
accessories just for lesbian weddings!

Right now, you can buy the clothes online at
FourteenStyle.com and find a great selection of clothes
in standard and boy fits, in sizes from 0 to 24. Everything

was designed with, and tested and fitted on, lesbian and gender-nonconforming folks. The fabrics are very wedding-appropriate — we even have clothes in velvet and linen.

And as for me at my wedding? Well, I was lucky. Banana Republic's 2009 line of summer suits included a line in white. I scored with the brand's Martin Fit trousers in white with a matching jacket. The trousers had a great flow to them and weren't too business-like. The fabric was light and soft to the touch, with a slight sheen. I totally lucked out, but I didn't find anything until May for a July wedding. Had I waited any longer, I wouldn't have had time to get something custom made, which (because of the cost) was my last resort.

TRANSGENDER TIP: If you plan to wear a wedding dress, don't stress yourself out in advance about sizing or how your body will fit into it. If you go to a bridal shop, the dress you end up with will be custom made for your body and for your wedding. There *is* a dress for you! You will find it and you will look beautiful!

Green Tip: Hemp wedding gowns used to be hideous, but now there are many stylish options. Check out www.GetConscious.com/Gownindex.html for some ideas for your gown and bridesmaid dresses. If you're environmentally aware, you might also consider a wedding dress and bridesmaid dresses that can be worn again. Some brides who are eco-conscious also repurpose a dress worn by their moms. Finally, there are some beautiful, organic-cotton dresses available. A good resource for those is TheCottonBride.com.

✔ Make Up Your Mind About Hair and Makeup

Many of our brides (and bridegrooms!) have said to us, "I feel like I should wear makeup, but I don't want to look like anyone other than myself. I don't want to be a princess!" All of this is perfectly okay, of course. The best solution is to try out several vendors and see who listens to you most closely. This is called a trial. Who is going to make you look like the best version of yourself?

Before seeking assistance with wedding hair and makeup, I advise couples to look at images for examples of hair and makeup that they like and think would be a good fit for their hair and features. They should bring those photos to their meeting with the hair and makeup stylist(s).

My first suggestion is always to ask your personal hairstylist whether he or she travels onsite for wedding hair. If you already have a relationship with that person, it's great to be able to have that familiarity and peace of mind on your wedding day. But just because she or he is your personal stylist doesn't mean you should skip a trial. Be sure to have her or him do a test run of your look for the wedding. Only approve it if it really represents how you want to appear on your big day.

Before you get in touch with potential stylists, you'll want to resolve the following questions:

Are you paying for hair and makeup for any members of your wedding party? This is a personal decision and is not required. Some couples pay for hair and makeup for their wedding party as a gift to them.

How many people need hair and makeup? The total number of people may include the two people getting married, family members, and wedding-party members. Regardless of whether you are paying for their hair and makeup services, you should ask your wedding party if they would like access to this service.

Do you want the stylist(s) to stay throughout the wedding to provide you with touch-ups? There is a premium for this service, of course.

Do you want hair and makeup to be done onsite where you are getting ready, or are you willing to travel to your stylist? I strongly advise against traveling for this service on your wedding day. Allow yourself to be pampered and let the vendors come to you!

During your trial styling, bring a camera and ask the following questions:

• What is the stylist's experience with hair and/or makeup for same-sex weddings?

• Does the stylist provide both hair and makeup, or one or the other?

• How many people can the stylist handle without bringing in an assistant?

• If either of you isn't looking for much hair or makeup assistance, is the stylist capable of restraint? You want to make sure he or she isn't going to overdo you.

• What time does the stylist arrive onsite on the wedding day?

- What's the order for hair and makeup for the wedding party?

- What brand of products does the stylist use?

- Does he or she ever stay throughout the event for touch-ups?

- How can you make sure that your hair/makeup will last throughout the event?

- How long does the stylist typically spend on makeup per person?

- Does the stylist provide airbrushing? (if applicable).

Transgender Tip: If you are a transgender bride, be sure to come out when calling hairstylists and makeup artists. Not only are you looking for someone who is comfortable with you, but you may also require someone who has experience styling hairpieces or applying makeup to transwomen.

After the trial, make sure you get photos taken of yourself sporting the finished product so you can compare it with your appearance after other trials. When you decide on just the right look you want, the photos that capture it will help you get excited about your wedding day!

Chapter 9
Six Months Out

Consider what kind of ceremony you want to have

Same-sex wedding traditions

Memorialize your covenant with a sacred document

Plan your vows and readings

What's in a name?

✔ Consider What Kind of Ceremony You Want to Have

My favorite part of a same-sex wedding is the wedding ceremony. Every same-sex wedding makes history. Each one is rare, historical, and beautiful! You might as well make yours perfectly reflect who you are as a couple.

There are some specific considerations that will apply to whatever type of ceremony you're planning. Talk through these options together before you do anything:

How nontraditional do you want to be? Many couples choose a nontraditional ceremony because they see this as an opportunity to place their own personal stamp on it — or because they want to adhere to new same-sex-wedding traditions. On the other hand, some couples feel more comfortable with a ceremony that is similar to what they grew up with.

Are you having a more formal or less formal ceremony? The ceremony's formality will have an impact on the music you choose, the way you proceed down the aisle or aisles, and how your guests experience the event. Informal ceremonies often mean that most of your guests (except for immediate family and grandparents) are standing for the duration of the ceremony.

Are there guests who may have difficulty standing for a long period of time? Obviously, if standing for a long time is a challenge for your guests, you may want to have a more formal ceremony or be sure to provide seating for these individuals if you're having a very informal ceremony where most of the guests stand.

Are you having a religious or spiritual ceremony? Are there any spiritual, religious, or cultural rituals you want to adhere to? If there are, then your wedding may need to be officiated by a minister, rabbi, or celebrant.

Are you having your ceremony in a place of worship? Some venues may have a central aisle, thereby limiting your processional options. I'll discuss place of worship options in greater detail below.

If not in a house of worship, where will the ceremony be held? Does your reception venue have a good space that is ceremony worthy? Can the ceremony be in front of a fireplace, mantel, a lovely bookcase that has important meaning for you, or even a beautiful staircase? If so, you can get away without a great deal of floral arrangements. Would the ceremony be outside? How will you designate the ceremony space? Do you imagine a wedding arch, an arbor, a *chuppah*, or something else? You'll want to make sure to frame the ceremony space.

How long do you want the ceremony to last? Do you truly want to be in and out? Is the reception more important to you than the ceremony? Are you uncomfortable being the center of attention? If you answered yes to the three preceding questions, you'll probably want to plan on a very short ceremony. In my experience, informal wedding ceremonies tend to be fewer than 10 minutes long, with more formal ceremonies lasting for 20 to 30 minutes.

What kind of music do you want to hear as you process and recess down the aisle(s)? Do you want an organist, or a DJ or band playing your favorite contemporary song? Would you like a trio of strings playing something traditional? Perhaps you have one or more very musically inclined guests who can perform ceremony music. Many of my clients choose a contemporary pop song that is played either by a few members of the band or by the DJ.

How many attendants are you having? Keep the size of your wedding party in mind when considering where your ceremony will be held. If it's at a place of worship, a larger wedding party should fit comfortably. If it's in a less traditional venue, or the same place you're having your reception, there may be size constraints.

Do you want to enter the ceremony together or separately? Does either partner want to be the center of attention, or feel like the "bride"? I've planned only one wedding in which the two brides did not enter at the same time or together. In that instance, one of the lesbian brides waited in the ceremony area for the other to process down the aisle. In most cases, the couple walks in together or enters at the same time from two separate directions.

Are you interested in being escorted by parents or family members? At our wedding, Jen was escorted by her parents and I was escorted by my brothers (my parents had passed). Do you want to be escorted by anyone at all?

Do you want there to be a seating area designated for each side of the family? Traditionally, one side of the aisle is for the bride's family and guests, and the other side is for the groom's. Same-sex weddings usually skip this tradition, but that doesn't mean that you have to. If you would like to seat guests in this manner, you should plan on having ushers.

Do you want ushers? As mentioned above, ushers are most often used when there's a bride's side and a groom's side. Most same-sex weddings do not have ushers escort guests, and many don't have ushers at all, unless they are asked to distribute ceremony programs.

Have your guests been to a same-sex wedding before? If most of your guests have never attended a lesbian wedding, they may be a little nervous or on edge. To put people at ease, you may consider having sparkling water and wine passed around before the ceremony begins. Offering beverages in advance happens so frequently that it's become a same-sex wedding tradition. It's a nice way to let your guests know that this is not your ordinary wedding — plus it takes the edge off!

Do you want to sign a sacred marriage document? In the Jewish tradition, the couple signs a *ketubah* (marriage contract) before the ceremony. Quaker couples sign a marriage certificate. In some same-sex weddings, the couple signs a foundation covenant, a beautiful memento of your wedding day.

Do you want to have a unity ritual? The traditional unity ritual features a unity candle, which is lit by two smaller candles. The primary candle symbolizes the two families coming together. Other unity rituals include a wine ceremony and a sand ceremony, all symbolizing two becoming one. In each case, there are two different kinds of wine or sand placed together in the same vessel.

Informal Weddings

I've planned many weddings at which the 50-plus guests stood for 10- to 20-minute wedding ceremonies. There was select seating for elderly family and friends but generally no more than 20 or so chairs up front. These types of weddings have a nice casual vibe to them, and often the marriage ceremony seems to unfold very organically. They are perfect for small guest counts or for couples who don't like being the center of attention.

Formal Religious Ceremonies

Those members of the clergy authorized to perform same-sex marriages include: some rabbis (who often require you to be a member of their temple), United Church of Christ ministers, Metropolitan Community Church ministers, Episcopal ministers in some churches (ask!), Lutheran ministers in some churches (ask!), Unitarian Universalist ministers, non-denominational ministers, interfaith ministers, and a few others.

Faiths Allowing Same-Sex Marriages

Jewish: Reform and Conservative Jewish synagogues embrace same-sex marriage, and rabbis can perform ceremonies.

Metropolitan Community Church: Churches in the Metropolitan Community Church fully embrace and welcome lesbian, gay, bisexual, and transgender people and allow for same-sex marriage.

Quaker: The willingness varies by meetinghouse, but there is some acceptance and performance of same-sex marriages among Quakers.

Unitarian Universalist: Unitarian Universalist churches are supportive of same-sex marriages; many have "open and affirming" congregations.

United Church of Christ: The United Church of Christ was the first mainstream Christian church to fully support same-sex marriage. UCC has over 5000 churches and more than one million members.

Faiths Allowing Limited Same-Sex Marriage

Episcopal: Episcopal dioceses are allowed to decide, on a case-by-case basis, whether to allow same-sex marriages. At a minimum, they will bless the ceremony without pronouncing the marriage or signing legal paperwork. Episcopal priests in Eastern Massachusetts and New York City can fully marry same-sex couples without conditions.

Lutheran: Lutheran churches are allowed to decide on their own whether they will perform same-sex marriage ceremonies — it's up to the individual church.

Methodist: The United Methodist Church will not conduct same-sex marriages and will not allow them to be held in their churches, though about 1200 Methodist clergy have agreed to break the rules (though I can't tell you where to find these particular ministers!).

Faiths Disallowing Same-Sex Marriages

Baptist: Southern Baptist and Conservative Baptist churches will not conduct same-sex marriages, nor will they allow them to be held in their churches. Some American Baptist churches are open and inclusive.

Catholic: The Catholic Church will not conduct same-sex marriage ceremonies or allow them to be held in their churches. The Catholic Church continues to fight the legal recognition of homosexual couples.

Presbyterian: The Presbyterian Church does not sanction same-sex marriage, and a Presbyterian minister cannot perform a same-sex union ceremony like the marriage ceremony.

✔ Same-Sex Wedding Traditions

There comes a time, and it may be just about now — nine years after the first same-sex marriages in the United States — when we take stock of LGBT wedding trends. At this point, we're starting to see some trends become same-sex-wedding traditions. Some of them are:

Preceremony Champagne

There's a strong and palpable feeling of triumph and celebration at LGBT weddings. But before that feeling actually sets in, many of the guests (particularly

those who have never before attended a same-sex wedding) simply don't know what to expect. The guests start out with a great deal of anticipation; they're a little nervous, excited, and curious. We like to help them relax, and so we recommend greeting them before the ceremony with Champagne and sparkling water. The refreshments may be served for 5 to 30 minutes before the ceremony begins, and this sets a fun and celebratory tone.

Some couples will have preceremony cocktails or a preceremony open bar . . . be careful with this, as it makes the guests harder to "herd," and it's more challenging to get them to focus when you are ready for the ceremony to start.

The Unique Processional

Many couples choose not to enter down one central aisle like straight brides do. Often, the partners walk in from two different directions, each accompanied by his or her family and/or wedding party, and the two meet in the middle.

The Ceremony Music

At same-sex weddings, pop songs are often featured. Sometimes, the piece is played live, and sometimes couples have the recorded version of the song played. Here are some common options:

- "All You Need Is Love" by the Beatles

- "Today" by Joshua Radin

- "In My Life" by the Beatles

- "Your Precious Love" by Marvin Gaye and Tammi Terrell

- "You Are the Sunshine of My Life" by Stevie Wonder

- "The Rainbow Connection" by Kermit the Frog

The Validation and Affirmation

Following the processional, the guests remain standing, Champagne in hand, for the opening remarks and tradition of "validation and affirmation," which is essentially a brief introductory blessing/toast led by the officiant and toasting you, the couple. Then, the guests sit and the ceremony proceeds.

The Foundation Covenant

Later in the ceremony, after the vows are exchanged, the officiant asks the couple to sign the foundation covenant. This document is inspired by the *ketubah*, the Quaker wedding certificate, and other such sacred marriage documents, and is an art piece signed by the couple and later by the guests. I work with one designer who creates foundation covenants that tie in to my client's custom wedding stationery. But foundation covenants are also sold through the Web site ModernKetubah.com. The designer, Daniel Sroka, creates beautiful fine-art pieces inspired by nature.

Ceremony Processional Options

There are many ways you can set up your wedding ceremony space (especially at a lesbian wedding, since there are no expectations of you!). The space can truly set the tone for your wedding. There are a number of processional options available to you, but the two main ones are:

THE CENTRAL AISLE

This conventional ceremony setup is what was often used at weddings at most churches or synagogues in the past. The chairs are arranged on either side of the

aisle. Most church or synagogue weddings nowadays, even same-sex weddings, use a central aisle. Sometimes, the chairs face directly ahead, and sometimes they're at an angle or in a semi-circle, but the concept is still the same — one aisle down the middle. In this scenario, the brides will most often process together, holding hands.

MULTIPLE AISLES

A multiple-aisle setup is designed to convey the "meet-in-the-middle" metaphor of two people becoming one. The way you arrange the two aisles depends on the venues you use. Sometimes you can have the aisles begin at either end of a row of chairs. Or you can have them form on the left and right sections of the ceremony space. Or you may want to have two parallel aisles in between three sections of chairs.

The Recessional

After the ceremony at many same-sex weddings, the couple recesses out to a contemporary/pop song.

✔ Memorialize Your Covenant with a Sacred Document

I love *ketubahs*, foundation covenants, and other sacred wedding documents. I think they are elegant and can reflect the personality of the couple. For example, at Sarah and Jane's wedding, the language on the *ketubah* was in Hebrew (because Sarah's Jewish), in Korean (because Jane's Korean American), and in English. And it was absolutely gorgeous!

Traditionally, the *ketubah* is signed by the couple, their rabbi/officiant, and a few witnesses before the wedding. The foundation covenant and the Quaker marriage certificate are signed by the couple and their officiant during the ceremony, and by their guests witnessing the covenant, after the ceremony. As I mentioned earlier, a foundation covenant can also substitute as a guest book.

We had a foundation covenant at our wedding, and it was produced by Daniel at Modern Ketubah, whose beautiful work completely exceeded our expectations. Our foundation covenant will grace the walls of our home, and will always remind us of the love and support of our friends and family.

✔ Plan Your Vows and Readings

A question I'm often asked by couples is, "Should we write our own vows?" Jen and I talked about it and decided not to write ours on our own. We figured that there were plenty of gorgeous vows out there — why reinvent the wheel when we might not be so eloquent?! But I must admit, I love it when I'm standing in the back of the room watching the couple reveal their deeply personal, handwritten vows to each other for the first time. There's almost nothing more moving.

If you choose not to write your own vows, don't worry: your minister, celebrant, or justice of the peace will have a good selection of choices for you. And if you are a little shy, you actually have the choice of not reading your vows aloud. Your officiant can say the vow in a form of a question and just ask you to say, "I do," so you can keep it short and sweet.

I'm including the vows Jen and I exchanged so you can see what spoke to our hearts. I'm sure you'll find words (perhaps these!) that will resonate as much for you:

> *Today I love you completely, as I did yesterday and will tomorrow. I will be there for you always. I will share in your dreams, delight in your joys, and comfort you in your sorrows. I will be your confidant, your counsel, and your friend. When you are not within my sight, you will be within my thoughts. You are my life, you are my joy; you are my love, and today, you are my wife.*

Religious Readings for the Ceremony

I know that some people, myself and Jen included, have difficulty reconciling their sexuality with the religious traditions that they grew up with (in our case, we both grew up Catholic). We know that there are many religious institutions that don't perform or recognize our marriages. The good news, though, is that there are some passages from the Bible and other sacred texts that may bring you comfort and that you may find appropriate for your wedding.

BIBLE READINGS

RUTH 1:16–17

But Ruth said, "Entreat me not to leave you or to return from following you; for where you go I will go, and where you lodge I will lodge; your people shall be my people, and your God my God; where you die I will die, and there will I be buried. May the Lord do so to me and more also if even death parts me from you."

1 CORINTHIANS 13:1–8A

If I speak in the tongues of mortals and of angels, but do not have love, I am a noisy gong or a clanging cymbal. And if I have prophetic powers, and understand all mysteries and all knowledge, and if I have all faith, so as to remove mountains, but do not have love, I am nothing. If I give away all my possessions, and if I hand over my body so that I may boast, but do not have love, I gain nothing. Love is patient; love is kind; love is not envious or boastful or arrogant or rude. It does not insist on its own way; it is not irritable or resentful; it does not rejoice in wrongdoing, but rejoices in the truth. It bears all things, believes all things, hopes all things, endures all things. Love never ends.

JEWISH BLESSINGS

Many Jewish couples, straight or gay, use the Seven Blessings. Here is a contemporary version of the Blessings:

THE JEWISH SEVEN BLESSINGS, CONTEMPORARY

May your marriage enrich your lives.

May you work together to build a relationship of substance and quality.

May the honesty of your communication build a foundation of understanding, connection, and trust.

May you respect each other's individual personality and philosophy, and give each other room to grow and fulfill each other's dreams.

May your sense of humor and playful spirit continue to enliven your relationship.

May you understand that neither of you is perfect; may your love strengthen when you fall short of each other's expectations.

May you be best friends, better together than either of you apart.

SECULAR READINGS

For those of you who prefer a nonreligious reading, here are a few that are popular:

THE APACHE WEDDING PRAYER

Now you will feel no rain, for each of you will be shelter for the other. Now you will feel no cold, for each will be warmth for the other.

Now you will feel no loneliness, for each of you will be companion to the other. Now you are two persons, but there are three lives before you: her life, your life, and your life together.

May beauty surround you both on the journey ahead and through all the years. May happiness be your companion to the place where the river meets the sun.

Go now to your dwelling to enter into the days of your life together. And may your days be good and long upon the earth.

"A SACRED SPACE" FROM THE *TAO TE CHING* BY LAO-TZU

Your love requires space in which to grow. This space must be safe enough to allow your hearts to be revealed. It must offer refreshment for your spirits and renewal for your minds. It must be a space made sacred by the quality of your honesty, attention, love, and compassion. It may be anywhere, inside or out, but it must exist.

OTHER GREAT READINGS

Some other popular readings you might want to consider include:

- "This Marriage — Ode 2667" by Rumi

- "Touched by an Angel" by Maya Angelou

- Excerpts from *Leaves of Grass* by Walt Whitman

- Excerpt from *The Prophet* by Kahlil Gibran

- "How Falling in Love Is like Owning a Dog" by Taylor Mali

Interestingly, the most popular reading at same-sex wedding ceremonies is not from a celebrated poet or inspirational novel, nor from a sacred text or a religious tradition. The most popular same-sex wedding ceremony reading has tremendous meaning. It's historical. It's beautifully written. It speaks volumes about the significance of a marriage. And it was written by a lawyer . . . well, a judge actually. The most popular reading during same-sex wedding ceremonies is part of the ruling that legalized same-sex marriage in Massachusetts (the first state to legalize same-sex marriage). It was written by Judge Margaret Marshall from the state Supreme Judicial Court. While this is by no means the whole ruling, the passage on the top of the next page is the excerpt most commonly used:

Marriage is a vital social institution. The exclusive commitment of two individuals to each other nurtures love and mutual support; it brings stability to our society. For those who choose to marry, and for their children, marriage provides an abundance of legal, financial, and social benefits. In return it imposes weighty legal, financial, and social obligations . . . Without question, civil marriage enhances the "welfare of the community." It is a "social institution of the highest importance."

Marriage also bestows enormous private and social advantages on those who choose to marry. Civil marriage is at once a deeply personal commitment to another human being and a highly public celebration of the ideals of mutuality, companionship, intimacy, fidelity, and family . . . Because it fulfills yearnings for security, safe haven, and connection that express our common humanity, civil marriage is an esteemed institution, and the decision whether and whom to marry is among life's momentous acts of self-definition.

✔ What's in a Name?

I was recently corresponding with a couple who sent me a note on their ceremony draft. One of the brides wrote, "Elizabeth and I have been together for more than 20 years. After a life of saying 'my partner,' I'd love, at long last, to say, 'my wife.'"

And so she did. Language is a funny thing. I know another unmarried lesbian couple who've been together more than 10 years, and they refer to themselves not as partners, but as lovers. That term is not for everyone but it works for them.

What words to use in referring to one another is a big decision for lesbian couples. I get asked all the time about how the officiant will "declare" them at the conclusion of the ceremony.

I now declare you . . .

- legally married
- partners for life
- wives to one another
- spouses for life
- lawfully married
- married partners
- wives
- [come up with language of your own]

Jen and I chose "legally married." That phrase felt right for me, because in my mind the legal element of the wedding is so important. We live in a state where our marriage is legal, and I want that word to be heard loud and clear. But that's not always the case, and not everyone wants the declaration to sound even remotely "political."

Once you're actually hitched, how will you refer to your spouse? Many couples I know initially cringed at using the word "wife." I had a hard time adjusting to the word "fiancée," and that took quite a while to feel natural. Many couples still use the term "partner" because it's what's comfortable and familiar. And to be perfectly honest, for the first few months after our wedding, I occasionally caught myself referring to Jen as "my girlfriend"! Whoops!

And finally, what about the last name? Many people keep their names, but I've had several clients and a friend invent entirely new names, some of which were not remotely similar to either of the old names. That's kind of fun — as you begin a new life together, you do so with a new name. And, of course, you can hyphenate your names. Sometimes this works out nicely (if the names flow together), but sometimes it's awkward.

So what did the wedding planner do? One hyphenated and one not. Jen wanted to use a hyphen and I did not, so Jen is now Jennifer Coveney-Smith and I am Bernadette Coveney Smith. We simply couldn't come to an agreement on the hyphen, so we agreed to disagree and are living happily with that decision.

Chapter 10
Five Months Out

Consider your catering needs and options
Schedule the all-important tasting
Decide on the bar
Choose your wedding cake

The next group of vendors you will hire are those who can generally provide services for more than one event per day. For example, it's not unusual for florists to have multiple weddings on an evening or over a weekend. They have the staff to make it happen. These vendors can be hired four to six months before the wedding, so the earlier you have their services secured, the better!

✔ Consider Your Catering Needs and Options

Our loved ones are still talking about how good the food was at our wedding. No boring, overcooked chicken for us. Our guests had lobster and filet mignon, and the food didn't cost an arm and a leg. Your guests are going to spend at least a good two hours eating at your wedding (including the cocktail hour), so you might as well give them something memorable. Before calling caterers, answer the questions below yourselves, as a couple:

How many guests do you expect at your wedding? You can provide a range, but by now you should have a good idea of how many to expect.

Are the ceremony and reception in the same location? This is an important issue for timing. If the ceremony is onsite, the caterer may have to set up earlier than normal so as to be well out of the way before guests begin to arrive. Depending on the venue, the caterer may also preset dinner tables and pull them to the side of the room to be screened off for the ceremony.

Are you serving Champagne or anything before the ceremony? Traditionally, same-sex couples greet their guests before the ceremony with butler-passed sparkling wine or water. This lets the guests know that this is not your ordinary kind of wedding and helps to set a festive mood at the very beginning.

What is your favorite kind of food? Are you a foodie, or do you like classic American comfort food? Do you have a favorite restaurant that is a special place for you both? Do you have a favorite ethnic food that's crucial to include on your wedding menu? We've had clients ask the caterer to base their wedding-dinner menu on that of one of their favorite restaurants.

Do you want to have a long cocktail reception, a buffet, food stations, a family-style meal, or a plated dinner? Let's explore this a bit. There are pros and cons to each, but the decision is often based upon the type of energy you want to create at your wedding.

Cocktail Reception

This is a big party with most guests standing and limited seating. To do this effectively, you should have a shorter event (otherwise guests might get bored or tired). You'll also want to make sure that you keep the food flowing all night so your guests feel as though they've eaten a proper meal. You also want to add an additional entertainment element (like a drag show or photobooth or something else) to make sure your guests don't get bored. Create a lounge area for your guests with tables and chairs (either provided by the venue or rented by you). This type

of wedding is casual and informal, but the cost of a cocktail-reception-style event is not necessarily much less expensive than a more structured party. You still have to provide a lot of food and staff.

Buffets and Food Stations

These are nice because they're casual, they get your guests out of their seats, and they provide an opportunity for mixing, mingling, and getting to know one another. You'll want to offer a greater variety of foods at a buffet or food station than you probably would at a plated dinner. Food stations can be themed or interactive. An example of this is a pasta station in which pasta is sautéed to order depending on the sauce or veggies chosen. In this scenario, guests are asked to go up to the buffet or stations, table by table, while everyone else must wait their turn. Typically, two to three tables at a time can go up. As a point of etiquette, the head table (or newlywed table) goes first, followed by immediate family.

Of course, a major downside to buffets and food stations is that not everyone eats at the same time, and some of your guests (for example, those at the last table to go up) may be waiting 45 minutes for food. Guests eat more at a buffet or food station, so food may run out (I've had this happen to me as a guest when my table was the last called to the buffet). A common misconception is that a buffet or food station will be less expensive than a plated meal. If it is, it's only slightly less expensive. Though caterers provide fewer staff for buffets or food stations, they have to provide more food. In the end, the prices of the two are fairly comparable.

Family Style

In this case, servers place large platters of food at each table and those platters are passed around among the guests, family style (just like it sounds). This type of service can be really nice in the sense that it creates intimacy. Although it sounds like a fun idea, in execution it doesn't work that well at weddings. There's not much table space for all of those platters, and the food cost ends up being high because so much food is provided.

Plated Dinners

These meals are served tableside by waitstaff that bring the food to you. Guests stay seated and there's little interaction with other tables. This is a more formal option. In general, there will be one first course (appetizer, soup, or salad) and one second course

(an entrée), followed by a cake course, although there may be even more courses depending on your style and budget. Generally, your guests will not get a choice of food for the first course and the cake course, but instead will be served something that you've preselected and believe to be universally appealing. A good caterer who is well staffed will set most of the meals within just a few minutes of one another. Plated dinners are, in my opinion, the most elegant way to feed your guests at a wedding reception, though you may find them slightly more expensive than the other options.

Do you want the caterer to provide the dessert or wedding cake? Many caterers have in-house pastry chefs who can prepare a variety of desserts for you, possibly even including a wedding cake. My favorite caterer in Boston has made the most magnificent wedding cakes for my clients. I'll never forget the one with mascarpone cream . . . mmmm.

Do you want the caterer to provide the bar, if that's an option with your venue? A full-service caterer should be able to provide you with a bartender, ice, and liquor-liability insurance, and should also be able to order the alcohol and mixers. In short, a full-service caterer can do it all. Some caterers just take care of food, however, and in those cases you'll have to hire a bartending service and work with a liquor store for the rest.

Do you want to ask guests to preselect their entrées? Prior to the wedding, the caterer will want to know how many of your guests will want a particular entrée. You can ask your guests to note on their invitation-response card the entrée options they would like. Then, you tell the caterer the number of each chosen entrée and, once you've set up table assignments, the number of each entrée at each dinner table. However, it's increasingly common not to ask your guests to choose their entrées in advance, but rather to present a small set menu at each place setting. On the menu, guests will see the preselected dishes for the first course and dessert course, and a short list of entrées to choose from as a second course. Here's an example:

First course:
Mixed Green Salad with Granny Smith Apples, Dried Cranberries and Chèvre

Second course:
Grilled Statler Breast with a Mushroom and Chestnut Sauce or Lemon-Glazed Grilled Scallops Served over Smoked Tomato and Fennel Puree, both served with Roasted Root Vegetables and Mashed Cauliflower Drizzled with Lemon-Chive Butter

Dessert:
Wedding Cake and Crème Brûlée

You should know that this set menu option is more expensive (an extra $5 to $10 per person) since the caterer has to be prepared to have more food on hand, and you will have to create and print a menu (if the caterer does not provide one).

Alternately, without any preselection or tableside ordering required, each guest can be given a plate with a dual entrée — that is, one of each, à la surf and turf. Some guests may just want the surf or the turf, however, and the caterer should be prepared to accommodate this request.

Once you've given serious thought to your own food and service desires, you can start researching caterers. These are the questions you should ask when first speaking with caterers (this list assumes that the wedding is in a place where you supply your own caterer):

• Is this an LGBT-owned business?

- Have you worked on any same-sex weddings before?

- Have you worked in [your venue] before?

- Are you a full-service caterer? Can you provide buffets, plated dinners, and food stations?

- Do you coordinate rentals, including linen rentals?

- Do you offer set menus or require all of your entrées to be preselected in advance? Can the wedding entrée be a duo of two proteins?

- Can you provide bartenders, liquor liability, ice, beer, wine, liquor, mixers, and other bar supplies?

- Do you make wedding cake or other desserts?

- Can you accommodate special dietary needs such as gluten-free, vegan, vegetarian, and/or nut-free meals?

At this meeting, the caterer should offer to put together a proposal for you. Once you've received a few proposals and made any changes to better suit your needs and/or budget, you can schedule a tasting.

✔ Schedule the All-Important Tasting

It's so important to taste the food you will eat on your wedding day. You should note that some caterers won't do a tasting unless you've already signed a contract with them. Some will charge a fee, around $50 or $100, that is credited toward your bill if you book with them. And some caterers or venues will schedule monthly or quarterly group tastings with their clients. Keep in mind that, in some cases, you'll be choosing a caterer before you actually get to taste the food. This is certainly not ideal, but you'll have to rely on your intuition, reviews, and how enthusiastic you are about the initial menu.

Whenever I'm working with clients, the tasting is one of my favorite parts of the planning process. Of course! Free food, yes, but the look in a couple's eyes when they actually sit down and taste the food they may be having on their wedding day is pretty special. Especially, of course, if it tastes good and they are comfortable and happy with the process. The tasting makes the wedding suddenly begin to feel real.

Your tasting should include at least a few hors d'oeuvres that are part of your most recent wedding proposal, as well as two or three samples from your first course, entrée, and side selections. If the caterer or venue is providing wedding cake, you should be able to taste that, too (though I prefer to go on cake tastings separately). An effective tasting should answer many of the questions about your wedding day and the flow of the event. Here are the things you should note about your tasting:

- How is the food presented?

- Are hot dishes served hot and cold dishes served cold?

- Is the plate presentation appetizing?

- Are the hors d'oeuvres easy for your guests to eat? Are you using skewers? I personally find them awkward and unattractive!

- Do the flavors pop? Are they complex? Is the food absolutely divine?

- Do the courses flow well together? Is there too much of one kind of protein, or do you have items that are very polarizing (like goat cheese, which I love)? I'm not saying you need to change or eliminate those items, just be aware not everyone will like them!

- Is there a nice balance of selections for vegetarians and carnivores?

- Will there be any in-season changes to the menu?

- If the caterer will be managing your rental order, ask whether the linens have been picked out. Make him or her show you swatches!

- Are the plates at the tasting the same plates you'll be using on your wedding day? Are the flatware and stemware the same?

- Will you be having decorative charger plates? Chargers are larger plates at each setting onto which your napkin, menu, and some or all food courses are placed. Say yes! Chargers are lovely!

- What is their standard napkin fold? Do you like it?

- Be sure to get assurance that every last person on the service staff will treat the two of you, as well as all your LGBT guests, with respect. Indicate that there's no place for homophobia at your wedding and reception!

- If you are choosing a set menu (rather than preselected entrées), does the caterer or venue provide menu cards? What is the heading at the top of the cards?

- Think about when you will be having a Champagne toast. Do you want the Champagne preset at the dinner table?

- What is the approximate timing for dinner? How long does it take the caterer to get through three courses if serving a plated meal?

- Is there a separate cake-cutting fee?

- Can the caterer provide tableside wine service? Do you want him or her to?

- Confirm whether the fee includes a staff gratuity. (A gratuity for the staff is typically not included when you are working with an outside caterer.)

- Confirm the bar setup if you are hosting the bar. Does the caterer charge a flat fee per person or by consumption — that is, what guests drink? (Maybe you'll be lucky enough to bring in your own alcohol.)

- If possible, taste your wedding wine with the food. If the venue provides the food and bar, then ask the staff for a wine tasting. If you're bringing in your own caterer and bar, then bring your own wine to the tasting!

- If you haven't already done so, arrange a location with the caterer for your gift table, guest book, and escort cards.

- If you don't have a wedding planner to manage the caterer, who will be your day-of-event go-to person? What authority does that person have to act as an event planner and liaison with the other vendors like the DJ and photographer?

✔ Decide on the Bar

There are so many debates over serving alcohol at a wedding. Whether or not to have a bar, and what to provide if you do, is full of controversial issues!

LET'S START WITH SOME DEFINITIONS:

Host/open bar: A host/open bar means that the hosts of the wedding pay for the bar and the guests do not. Host bars are typically charged on consumption or at a flat rate per guest. A host bar can be either a full bar (described below) or a limited, signature bar.

Cash bar: At a cash bar, guests pay for their own alcoholic drinks.

Full bar: A full bar means that guests may choose from a full choice of beers, wines, and alcoholic drinks. This can be a host/open bar or a cash bar.

Limited bar: Guests may choose from a limited selection of alcoholic drinks, which typically include a red or a white wine, several beers, and one signature cocktail.

HERE ARE SOME HELPFUL HINTS ON MANAGING THE BAR SITUATION — AND YOUR BAR BUDGET:

- Create a signature drink. Signature cocktails are a great way to personalize your wedding. Your signature drink might relate to your color theme, the season, your favorite spirit, or something else entirely — whatever you choose, it's nice to have a fun signature cocktail that reflects your personality. You can rename a popular drink with something more representative of the two of you. For example, you could have a signature cocktail called the "Ptown Partini" if you were having your wedding in Provincetown or having a beach-themed wedding. Even if you don't provide a full bar, offering a signature cocktail is classy and a great conversation starter. Plus, having a signature drink but no other liquors can lower your overall alcohol budget, because many guests will switch to typically lower-priced beers and wines.

- It's a nice idea to offer a signature "mocktail" for your nondrinking guests (who may enjoy something more interesting than a club soda with lime).

- Although toasts are traditionally with Champagne or sparkling wine, you can certainly do a "toast-in-hand" instead. Many people don't even like Champagne!

- Tip jars are confusing and fairly tacky, so don't have one at the bar at your wedding!

✔ Choose Your Wedding Cake

I'm hungry already. I am a firm believer that wedding cake should be delicious and need not be dry, cold, or sugary. The best cake-makers book up well in advance, so don't procrastinate about this delicious process! Small cake shops generally limit themselves to making 10 or fewer wedding cakes per weekend, while larger shops can handle many more. To get you started in selecting a wedding cake, there are a few "terms of art" you should know:

Buttercream: Buttercream is a smooth, creamy frosting made out of butter. It tastes great, is easy to serve, and can be piped to decorate the cake.

Fondant: Fondant is a type of icing generally made out of sugar, corn syrup, and gelatin. It's rolled with a rolling pin into a thin sheet that gets draped over the cake. It has a smooth, nonsticky finish, and can be painted, colored, and decorated with virtually anything. Most people don't like the taste of fondant, but because buttercream is generally under it, I ask my caterers to remove the fondant prior to cutting and serving it to guests so the cake tastes its best, with just the buttercream. Fondant is easily removed. Note that fondant makes the cake more expensive.

Ganache: Ganache is a sweet, rich chocolate, more dense than mousse but less dense than fudge, which can be used as icing or filling.

Filling: The filling is the yummy goodness between each layer. Filling flavors include lemon, raspberry (or other fruits), coconut, chocolate mousse, and lots more.

Taste the Cake!

Naturally, one of my favorite parts of wedding planning is cake tasting, and I've had plenty of wedding cake in my many years of planning same-sex weddings. It never gets boring to me. Be sure you go on several cake tastings before you make your final decision. The taste can vary widely. Some buttercreams are gritty and overly sugary. Some cakes themselves are dry. Fondant almost universally tastes bad — but looks great! I'm sure I don't have to convince you, but *taste the cake!* It's fun.

Cake Prices

Wedding cakes are almost universally priced by the slice, typically $3 and up per slice, depending on the décor. Fondant and heavily decorated cakes (à la Cake Boss of Boston) are more expensive because of the time required for decorating. These could easily be $10 and more per slice. Serving cupcakes can be slightly more cost effective, depending largely on their size. They are typically $2 and up per unit.

Prettying the Cake

If you are not going to get elaborate with the design of the cake, I recommend using fresh flowers to decorate an otherwise simple cake. If you do this, be sure to identify whether the florist or baker is in charge of this detail. If it's the florist, confirm that the delivery person puts the flowers on the cake, or assign someone else to do it. If it's the cake designer, he or she will take care of the fresh flowers when the cake arrives. One way or another, make sure you have a plan for this.

Questions for the Bakery

When you start contacting bakers, be sure to ask the following questions:

- Is this an LGBT-owned business?

- Do you have experience with same-sex weddings?

- How many flavors of cake and filling can we taste at the tasting?

- What's the delivery fee?

- Can I see a portfolio?

While at the tasting, take the opportunity to ask:

- Do you make custom-designed cakes?

- Do you have "stock" designs?

- How many days prior to the wedding do you make the cake?

- How long prior to the wedding start-time do you deliver the cake?

- How many cakes do you produce in a weekend?

- What ingredients do you use?

- How many servings are there per tier of cake?

- Do you offer fresh flowers as a garnish?

- Do you provide an anniversary cake?

- Do you offer desserts in addition to cake?

- Do you sell cake toppers?

Options Instead of a Wedding Cake

A recent trend has been for couples to have wedding desserts that aren't really wedding cakes. Sometimes this is because they are having a nontraditional wedding and prefer an amazing dinner-party experience with the pastry chef's best desserts. And sometimes it's because everyone seems to think cupcakes and pies are more fun. Whatever the reason, it's now very common to have supplemental desserts in addition to (not instead of) a gorgeous, delicious wedding cake.

Cake-Cutting Tips

Some couples have the cake served at a coffee-and-cake station rather than brought to each table. I like this idea because it gets your guests up and out of their seats and can encourage more mingling and interaction (it also helps get them on the dance floor). Another advantage of a cake station is that not everyone eats cake, and therefore you can order up to 10 percent less than your actual guest count.

If you prefer multiple desserts from your favorite bakeries, you can still keep the fun cake-cutting tradition at your reception. Just cut the blueberry pie or strawberry shortcake!

Chapter 11
Four Months Out

Figure out your floor plan
Decide on your overall wedding design
Focus on invitations

You've reached the stage where your wedding is almost planned. The major logistics are done: the officiant, photographer, videographer, florist, and cake-maker are booked. Now, how do you make the event look, feel, and flow well? The flow starts with the room where most of your wedding activity will occur. Let's call that room the ballroom, even if it's not.

✔ Figure Out Your Floor Plan

Most couples don't spend much time thinking about their reception floor plan or room layout. And it's not something that is discussed in many wedding-planning books. Although the floor plan isn't very glamorous, it's a critical element in ensuring a smooth and fun reception, especially if you're having a seated meal rather than a cocktail reception. It's all about the flow, and if the room is crowded or your guests are in lines, they will definitely notice, and that's what they'll remember!

Accommodate Guests with Special Needs

If you have any guests who are in a wheelchair, who have trouble moving, or who have larger bodies, assign them to a table that won't be in a high-traffic area. You don't want them to have to be constantly moving their chair in order to let other guests pass by.

✔ Decide on Your Overall Wedding Design

I think of basic wedding design in four main areas: chairs, tablescapes (which are creatively designed tables), lighting, and floral decoration.

Chairs with Flair

When your guests walk into your space, chances are they'll see a sea of chairs . . . the sheer quantity you'll need makes them an important visual element. We've all been to ballrooms where the standard chair is something that's not quite wedding-appropriate, looking more suitable for an eight-hour corporate meeting (and in fact designed for that purpose). Sure, you can use those chairs at your wedding, but will they fit the overall look you seek? You can cover them up with chair covers, but most clients I've worked with don't bother covering the standard ugly banquet chairs with

(nearly as tacky!) chair covers. Instead, they bring in new chairs altogether.

The most common chair style, by far, is the ballroom or chiavari chair. Available in a wide variety of colors and seat-pad colors, it can match any décor. It's elegant, sturdy, and comfortable, and you can rent them for about $7 or $8 each. But $7 per chair can add up, and if you choose to use chair covers instead, those are about $4 each. While not as elegant as the chiavari chair, they are certainly better than those ugly banquet chairs. Outdoor and tented weddings typically have the garden chair, and these can be rented for $4 to $5 each.

Tablescapes

Table linens play a major role in creating your desired ambiance for an event. They can reinforce a theme and establish a cohesive feel. And you can give your reception tables some pizzazz without spending a lot of money. Most venues provide standard poly-cotton or plain cotton ivory or white linens, but most of my clients elect to upgrade to something nicer, using one of those fabrics but in a more thematic color. Besides lighting, upgrading linens is the single investment that will have the greatest visual impact at your wedding.

Also, table runners are very popular right now and can be made from discount fabrics, burlap, wallpaper, or whatever your imagination will allow. Don't overlook the napkins! Some linens have matching napkins, but often you'll use a poly-cotton or linen napkin that's the closest color you can find. I'm a big fan of napkin rings, and a rolled napkin adds an elegant touch.

Once you have these basic elements in place, you'll want to add china, stemware, and flatware. If you are bringing in your own caterer and renting items, you should ask to see samples so you can select the combination that best expresses your wedding vision!

It's All in the Lighting

First of all, why use lighting design for your wedding? Great lighting creates a mood. It can be virtually any color to match your theme. It can hide ugly walls. It creates ambiance and intimacy. It's romantic. Special lighting is no longer very expensive, and it can save you money in other areas (such as on flowers, perhaps). Here are a few of the most popular kinds of professional lighting.

UPLIGHTING

Uplights are placed on the floor and radiate color upward. Simple enough. You may have seen uplights at an event and not even noticed them. They are available in wired and wireless options — and the wired ones are nonheat-emitting LED lights. The lights can change colors throughout the night and can make a dramatic visual statement at a relatively low cost.

Many DJ and entertainment companies provide simple uplight packages for less than $1000 when booking their other services. It's a great investment.

PAPER LANTERNS

Most often seen outside or in tents, paper lanterns can be strung across any ceiling structure or a structure with a drop ceiling. Paper lanterns come in many different colors and even different shapes and are great for adding a casual, fun atmosphere at the wedding, and drawing the guests' eyes upward.

PIN SPOTS

Pin spots are little lights that highlight the dinner table from above. They shine directly down onto the centerpiece to make the table more romantic and intimate.

Say It with Flowers

The quickest and simplest way to decorate a space is through flowers. Jen is good at keeping our house full of flowers, candles, and music. I noticed this early on in our relationship, and it had such an impact on me that I made sure to mention it in our wedding ceremony. I love flowers.

A container (the florists often don't say "vase") of fresh flowers and greens instantly warms up a room, bringing oxygen and color. Weddings, of course, can be over-the-top with flowers, but there are some ways to keep it simple. Here are some important points when first considering your wedding flowers:

What are your wedding colors and themes? The florist will want to know this so he or she can suggest flowers accordingly.

What is your budget for flowers? In general, I suggest to couples that, for a wedding with 50 guests, you can count on spending between $1200 and $1500 on flowers. For 100 guests, expect to spend around $2000 to $2500 and up. This budget largely depends on the space you are using and how much it needs to be decorated.

What's your style? Some floral designers have a specific style. Some really shine at fluffy, ruffly, monochromatic designs (a very classic look), while others do their best work with textured, gardeny designs (to convey a rustic, garden-chic ambience). Still others are at their best with contemporary designs featuring exotic flowers. It's a great idea to clip images of floral designs you like or make a Pinterest board. Figure out what you're going for, and make sure you find the designer who excels at achieving that particular style.

Are flowers needed for the wedding party and for family members? Personal flowers include bouquets, nosegays (mini bouquets), corsages, and boutonnieres.

Will you designate your ceremony area with flowers? If you think about a traditional wedding ceremony, it's often held in front of an altar or under a *chuppah*. If you choose to do something else, it's always a nice idea to somehow designate the space as a sacred ceremony space, and it's usually the florist who provides the flowers and ceremonial elements. However, if your ceremony is in front of a fireplace, mantel, attractive bookcase, or even a beautiful staircase, you can get away without a lot of floral additions.

Choose flowers that will be in season on your wedding day and will last a day or two once cut. Your florist will be able to help you with this information. I love hydrangeas, for example, but they wither within a few hours of being out of water. They get thirsty, and thus might not be a great choice for a wedding bouquet that's going to be out of water all day.

Remember that floral design is hard work. It's more than just cutting flowers and putting them in a container. Flowers need to be picked, shipped, cut, have their leaves removed, and in some cases, be dethorned. They have to be treated for a few days to open up to their fullest. They have to be kept in a cool place. So it's a good idea to keep in mind that you're not only paying for the cost of the flowers but also for all the effort on the florist's end — the design, refrigeration, trucking, overhead (including insurance), and more.

Select a Florist

Once you've come up with a floral budget and an idea of your needs, it's time to call around for proposals. You should ideally contact two or three vendors and ask the following questions:

- Is this an LGBT-owned business?

- Have you worked with same-sex couples before?

- Do you require a minimum floral budget?

- Have you worked in [our venue] before?

Once you've made a short list of potential florists, you can set up a time for an in-person consultation. For these meetings, prepare yourself to ask the floral designer specific questions on the following points:

- Where do you source your flowers?

- Do you provide candles, linens, or other decorative items? In other words, are you an event designer?

- Do you rent floral containers or do we keep them?

- Do you rent any ceremonial elements, such as arches, a *chuppah*, or pedestals?

- Do you prepare a sample centerpiece close to the wedding date?

- What is the delivery and setup charge?

✔ Focus on Invitations

Having booked a venue and officiant and settled upon all of your major vendors, it's time to focus on invitations. By now, you've decided whom to invite. Even if you go with whimsical save-the-date cards, keep in mind that invitations truly set the tone for your wedding. If possible, you should use your wedding colors and/or theme on the invitations. The save-the-dates and invitation can be "teasers," giving your guests an advance preview of what they may expect on your wedding day.

What I like about the invitation is that it can be part of a cohesive theme that is carried throughout your wedding stationery: on the ceremony program, escort cards, table-name signs, menus, and so on. How cool to see a seamless design throughout. It's actually very efficient (and as a planner, I love efficiency) because it instantly conveys the décor. And I'm a big fan of green weddings, so even if you skip the ceremony program and the menu, you can still have a cohesive design theme.

Because it will take a while to have the invitations printed, you'll need to come up the design for them at this stage, to allow for plenty of time. They don't actually go in the mail until six to eight weeks before the wedding.

Before you go invitation shopping, ask yourself these important questions:

What is your budget for invitations? You can find invitations online for less than $2 per set, but the price can (literally!) go up to $30 or more per set. Many couples spend between $5 and $10 per set.

What is your color and/or theme? Start with one or both of these items and weave those design elements into your invitations, your ceremony program, your dinner menu, your escort and/or place cards, your table-name signs, and your thank-you notes.

Do you want a custom design? If you have a very specific theme and don't think you'll be able to find invitations in stores or online that reflect it, you can hire a designer to do custom artwork for you. It's what most of my clients do for results that are truly one of a kind.

What is the vibe of your wedding? If your invitation is traditional and elegant, your guests will assume it's a traditional and elegant wedding. Conversely, if your invitation is more fun and casual, your guests will expect that to be the vibe at your ceremony and reception.

Do you want to go shopping for invitations at a store so you can touch and feel them? Or would you rather sit behind your computer and purchase invitations online? The bonus of ordering online is that there's an enormous variety of options available. Also, you don't necessarily have to come out each time. You can also get samples sent to you from most major online invitation makers.

Do you want invitations that have lesbian imagery? By this I mean, do you want invitations that show silhouettes of two brides, or feature any kind of rainbow symbolism? If you do, then you should consider looking for them at a Web site such as GayWeddings.com or OutVite.com.

Stationers

You've probably heard of the stores Papyrus and the Paper Source, which are examples of national stationers that sell wedding invitations. There are also many independent stationers across the country that can help you achieve the kind of look you want for your wedding invitations. When you visit with stationers, you'll be able to see and touch many different kinds of wedding invitation styles. They will have giant books of invitations to choose from, with various customization options. Here are some things to ask when meeting with a stationer:

- How long is the turnaround time for an invitation suite?
- What types and/or font options can I choose from?
- What ink-color options can I choose from?
- How many different colors can an invitation suite contain?
- Can you show me examples of different print methods?
- Do you provide assembly and mailing service?
- Do you provide a calligraphy service?

Stationers, whether they are in storefronts or online, also may make custom designs. For example, the company I use most often, Ladyfingers Letterpress in Rhode Island, provides mostly custom stationery (with a small online store). For my clients' wedding at a wedding venue that used to be a summer camp, the ladies at Ladyfingers made beautiful custom designs with mountains in the background. For other clients of mine who had a wedding inside a townhouse with a fun-house theme, they made save-the-date cards with a fortune teller. You just can't buy that kind of creativity in stores!

The Envelope, Please

The invitation: This is the largest element, and it includes the names of the couple, the location of the wedding, and the date and time, as well as the names of parents (if they are hosting) and requested attire. It should *not* include the RSVP, registry information, or a wedding Web site URL. This information appears on the logistics card.

The logistics card: This card conveys information about other wedding-weekend activities, the URL of your wedding Web site, directions, and so forth. I tell my clients who are not inviting children to their wedding to state "Adults-Only Reception" or use similar language on their logistics card, and to include an offer to coordinate child care.

The RSVP card or postcard: This should be provided with a stamp or stamped envelope. The reply card is for guests to indicate whether they will attend and, in some cases, to select their entrée choice. Sometimes, the card will ask guests to mark whether they will participate in other wedding-weekend activities.

Directions: These may be on the logistics card, or if very detailed, they may require a separate enclosure, which may be a color map.

Tissue paper: This is often used to separate the invitation from the rest of the invitation suite.

For Better or for Verse

My favorite online resource for invitation verses is VerseIt.com. You'll be able to choose from a variety of verses depending upon your special circumstances. Your invitation may (or may not) set forth the involvement of parents, whether there are children involved, whether it's a destination wedding, and other such information. Here's what Jen and I used on our wedding invitation (below left).

Jennifer Marie Coveney

and

Bernadette Mary Smith

joyfully invite you to share

in their celebration of marriage

on Friday, the third of July

two thousand and nine

at six-thirty in the evening

The Exchange Conference Center

212 Northern Avenue

Boston, Massachusetts

Reception will immediately follow

Note that we chose the words "joyfully" and "celebration" because we wanted to immediately communicate that this was to be a big, fun party.

Invitation Etiquette

There are a lot of details to keep in mind as you mail out your invitations. Some of the most common questions I get are:

When should I mail the invitations? You should mail your invitations about six to eight weeks before the wedding (definitely eight weeks if you have a B-list or are sending invitations overseas).

When should I request a response? Request a response within four weeks of the wedding date. For example, if the wedding is July 1, ask for a response no later than June 8.

Who gets an invitation? Each unmarried adult guest should receive his or her own invitation even if they are roommates, siblings, or BFFs.

Do the names of children appear on the envelope? If you are inviting children, the names of the children should be on the outer envelope.

What goes on an invitation? As I mentioned earlier, your invitation itself is simply an invitation and should not include any of the items described above for the logistics card.

Do I need two envelopes, an outer and an inner? Traditionally, the invitation is in an envelope within an envelope. The original reason for this was to keep the inner envelope clean when invitations were hand delivered on horseback. Now you can get away with just one envelope (and save a tree).

Do invitations need to be hand addressed? Hand-addressed invitations are the tradition, and they are what many of the more conventional members of your guest list will expect. I am giving you permission to use nicely typed mailing labels (preferably clear) if you must.

Do the invitations need to be hand cancelled at the post office? If you have invested in expensive invitations, then yes, they should be hand-cancelled for gentler processing so they do not get beat up by post office machinery.

Web Resources

If it's easier for you to shop online than in a store, my favorite sites for wedding invitations are:

- GayWeddings.com
- OutVite.com
- LadyfingersLetterpress.com
- WeddingPaperDivas.com

You may need to ignore heterosexist language that you might find on some of these sites, but even if you do encounter it, I promise you that all of these sites are LGBT-friendly.

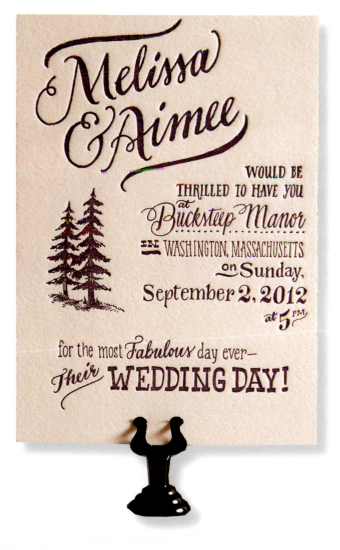

Chapter 12
Three Months Out

Get your rings!
Personalize your wedding
The run-up to the wedding
After the big event
Make your out-of-town guests feel welcome
Finalize the music
Plan for transportation

✔ Get Your Rings!

It's time to think about your wedding bands. As with everything, you are only limited by your imagination! So while there is no standard "lesbian engagement ring" or "lesbian wedding band," this can be one of the first areas where you as a couple can express your personality through your wedding.

I've seen rings that were mirror images of each other, rings that had a fingerprint imprinted on them, rings that were formed from family jewelry, and simple platinum or steel bands.

Some couples who already wear commitment rings will use those as their wedding bands as well. They'll simply move the ring to their right hand throughout the engagement and move it back to the left at the wedding. Other couples use their current commitment ring as an engagement ring, which then moves to the right hand after the wedding, when the new wedding band is worn on the left hand.

Whatever decision you choose, walking into a jewelry store with your fiancée and looking for a wedding band can be intimidating to say the least, particularly if you would

like a nontraditional band. Call around ahead of time to gauge the attitude of your local jewelers about working with same-sex couples. Or look around online to identify LGBT-friendly jewelers in your area. But still, call first. They may be great, or you may encounter an awkward pause, or even outright homophobia. If you do have a great phone call, make sure you catch the name of that associate so that you can work with the right person when you stop by the store.

✔ Personalize Your Wedding

As you think through these tips and options, keep in mind that it's your wedding, your day. It can be as personal as you wish. In addition to custom stationery, a thoughtfully created ceremony, inspired décor, and clever seating arrangements (we'll get to those in the next chapter!), here are some more areas in which your wedding can be personalized.

Wedding-Cake Toppers

If you choose to have a wedding cake with a cake topper, you can find some good resources for custom-made cake toppers that look just like you! A quick Internet search will reveal some good resources. I also recommend GayWeddings.com and shopping around for vendors on Etsy.com.

Guest Books

As mentioned earlier, many same-sex couples have their guests sign a foundation covenant instead of a guest book. In my experience, guest books usually end up with only a few pages written on and many blank pages. I don't really like them or recommend them. When thinking about a guest book, I try to imagine where it will be stored after the wedding. When will you look at it again? Will it just be collecting dust somewhere? One of the reasons I like the foundation covenant so much is that it's framed and hung on the wall.

Garters

To be honest, I've never seen a lesbian wedding with a garter toss, but I do think it's a fun tradition, and of course, I've had several brides wear garters. If you are interested in wedding garters, I highly recommend the collection by Julianne Smith, a DC-based designer of custom-made and stylish wedding garters. There can be elements of your parent's wedding incorporated, your favorite sports team, hobby, or anything else that has meaning to you. Julianne's collection is at TheGarterGirl.com.

Favors

In my opinion, favors should be done right or not at all! Go big or go home! After cleaning up after countless weddings where favors are left behind by guests enjoying themselves on the dance floor, I really believe that, in general, they're a waste.

That said, I've found the most successful favors are edible! Give guests a delicious truffle or chocolate-covered strawberry and it'll be gone, sometimes before the end of the night! Some edible favors can be packaged in such a way that the fold can double as an escort-card holder. In this case, the favor is placed on an escort-card table and guests bring it to their seat.

Another way to make sure that favors get distributed is to have them passed to guests as they exit. In the same way that Champagne is served to guests when they arrive, favors can be butler-passed on nice serving trays as guests leave. So classy!

DIY

DIY stands for "do-it-yourself." I'll be the first to admit that I'm not a crafty person and not at all adept at DIY projects. Some people, however (including, of course, Martha Stewart), are brilliant. There are some wonderful DIY resources you should check out to help you make napkin rings, guest books, escort cards, place cards, table runners, linens, and other wedding accessories. If you have the time, energy, and inclination to make a go at some DIY projects, I highly recommend the following Web sites for templates and step-by-step instructions:

- DIYBride.com
- MarthaStewartWeddings.com
- WeddingChicks.com

And if you, like me, are not a DIY master (but you still appreciate the handcrafted look), you'll find many cool wedding accessories for sale on Etsy.com. I know that I've recommended this site earlier in this chapter, but I think it's worth another mention. Etsy is a great place where crafters sell their wares and can even create custom products just for you. I've had some good experience with Etsy vendors, but be sure to read reviews and find out for yourself. On Etsy, you can purchase anything from napkin rings to aisle runners to invitations to wedding wardrobe. The variety is truly astounding!

✔ The Run-up to the Wedding: *The Wedding Rehearsal*

You have to have a wedding rehearsal. Even if it's only 15 minutes long, do it. Take the time to do a dry run so that you have fewer nerves on your wedding day.

Whom to invite: For your rehearsal, you and your partner should invite the wedding party, parents, grandparents, and readers. If possible, any musicians who will play at the ceremony should also attend. Do not invite anyone not involved in the wedding to the rehearsal, as they'll be distracting. This is not the time to be social!

Who's in charge: The officiant is in charge of the rehearsal, unless you have a wedding planner.

When: Preferably, the rehearsal should take place during the late afternoon or early evening before your wedding. *Tip*: Tell those who are invited to show up 15 to 30 minutes before you actually want the rehearsal to start. Some rehearsals are quite complex, and it's hard to catch up if you're running late!

Where: If possible, rehearse at your ceremony site. If you absolutely cannot use that location, I like small hotel function rooms and backyards as backup locations. But be sure to let all those coming know where it is!

How: If possible, arrange to have the room at least partly set up for the rehearsal so the processional and recessional can be accurately rehearsed and so everyone will know where to stand. If you are using a unity candle or foundation covenant, be sure to have a table set up by the ceremony site. If you are using a *chuppah*, it would be ideal to have this preset as well.

Tip: Meet your bridal party the night before or earlier in the day before the rehearsal so you can all go to the rehearsal together and no one will be late.

The Rehearsal Dinner

A trend I've seen lately is to invite to the rehearsal dinner all of the traveling guests who are in town on the night before the wedding. That's up to you, but that decision can balloon a 20-person rehearsal dinner to a 40-person rehearsal dinner. Double the number of guests and you double the budget.

In a traditional bride-and-groom scenario, the rehearsal dinner is hosted by the grooms' parents. You can make whatever arrangements work for you. The couple sometimes hosts, or one of the parents do, or it's a shared endeavor. But one way or another, it's nice to feed people. A rehearsal dinner need not be a formal affair. Sometimes, it's a cookout or a potluck. Choose an option that fits your budget and makes the most sense for you.

We decided only to invite those in our immediate family and in the wedding party to the rehearsal dinner. That meant we had about 20 guests. We wanted to create a casual, informal feel, so our rehearsal dinner was a gourmet pizza and salad buffet. The food was delicious and it was light and easy.

The Welcome Reception

Instead of a rehearsal dinner, many of my clients host a welcome reception/cocktail party for all the guests visiting. It's very informal, short (only about two hours), and often in the host hotel. There are usually no toasts and nothing structured. It's just a fun way to catch up with your wedding guests who have come from all over to be with you.

The Post-Rehearsal Dinner Party

To avoid the awkwardness of accommodating guests from out of town who arrive to your wedding location the night before the event, you should invite everyone to meet you at a central location for a casual get-together. For example, on the logistics card of our wedding invitation, we included the following:

> *Friday, July 2, 2009: At 8:00 p.m., please join us for live Irish music and drinks at Mr. Dooley's Irish Pub [address]*

This type of casual, welcoming invite does not obligate you to host this secondary event, but provides a common and casual meeting place for wedding guests. Just don't stay out too late or drink too much the night before your wedding!

✔ After the Big Event: *The Post-Wedding Brunch*

Even if you've already flown off on your honeymoon, the post-wedding brunch is another way to give wedding guests from out of town a way to be entertained.

Often, this brunch is hosted by the parents of the bride or groom, but the trend is to have it hosted by no one. Many couples simply spread the word verbally or include information in the guests' welcome bag (see the last section of this page below) to meet for brunch at a certain time. in the hotel restaurant. It's a painless and simple way to plan a brunch, and there's no financial obligation. And if you are, in fact, still around, your guests will appreciate seeing you again.

✔ Make Your Out-of-Town Guests Feel Welcome

Your guests may be traveling from many different parts of the country (or the world) to attend your wedding. You'll want to make sure they feel welcome during their stay. All it takes is a little extra planning to ensure that they're given the attention they deserve!

Tourist Activities

If your wedding is somewhere that is a true "destination" — that is, somewhere your guests may enjoy exploring as tourists — then it would be generous of you to provide them with a list of things to do. This could be as simple as typing up a bulleted list, or (if you feel like putting in a little extra effort) you could research the price of activities and phone numbers. You can also include local tourist information and maps, which are easily obtained at any hotel. However, you are under no obligation to set up tours, arrange meals, or purchase tickets.

As mentioned in the chapter about involving your parents, I'd advise that you delegate this task to a parent. It's one less thing for you to do and one more way to channel a parent's energy.

Welcome Bags

Speaking of DIY, if you expect to have many guests traveling in from out of town to attend your wedding, you may consider providing welcome bags or baskets to greet them in their hotel. This can be something you (or your mom or dad) can make yourself or you can buy many premade welcome bags online. My favorites are through my friend Kate Parker's site: KateParkerDesigns.com/welcome-bags.

If you are making your own welcome bags, these are some good things to include:

- a schedule of the weekend's events with transportation information, if applicable

- a tourist map of the area

- brochures (or preferably a tailored list of your suggested tourist stops)

- a snack or two (local delicacies are ideal!)

- bottles of water

You may also consider adding some hangover remedies!

Again, this is a really great project for Mom or Dad because it keeps them busy and lets them feel like they are hosting your guests.

✔ Finalize the Music

At this point, you should already have your DJ, band, drag queen, string quartet, karaoke superstar, line dancers, or whomever else you are hiring for your wedding entertainment. Now you have to figure out what to ask them to sing, play, or perform.

My advice here is simple: give them a little direction but let them do their jobs.

Carefully choose songs for the following, where applicable:

- processional song

- ceremony interlude song

- recessional song

- presenting brides (and possibly the wedding party) at the reception lunch or dinner

- first dance

- dance with any parents or family

- cake cutting

- any special songs (e.g., for drag performance)

- last dance

You can help your DJ or band out by putting together a simple list of your favorite artists or bands and any songs you *don't* want to hear at your wedding. Since I was an especially picky bride, I'm including my own "Do Not Play" list here for your own reference:

Bernadette's DO NOT PLAY List

"When a Man Loves a Woman"	"Rock This Town"	"Old Time Rock n' Roll"
"Mickey"	"Electric Avenue"	"My Girl"
"Cha Cha Slide"	"Hot Hot Hot"	"Chicken Dance"
"YMCA"	"Whip It"	"Super Freak"
"Limbo Rock"	"Mony Mony"	"Play That Funky Music"
"Conga"	"Le Freak"	"Love Shack"
"Brick House"	"Macarena"	"Celebration"
	"Electric Slide"	"Stayin' Alive"

✔ Plan for Transportation

I've noticed that same-sex wedding transportation rarely involves limos, stretch Hummers, or Rolls-Royces. Why? Traditionally, those vehicles are used to transport the wedding party to the ceremony and then to the reception. But when there's no wedding party and the ceremony and reception are in the same location, no limos are needed! It's a great way to save money.

But, you may find yourself in a situation where you have to provide guest transportation. This can be a huge expense. Big, 50-passenger charter buses can easily cost $600-plus, but they may not hold a lot more than some more whimsical vehicles. For example, when my clients need to provide guest transportation, instead of booking charter buses, I rent trolleys. These are easy to rent in Boston and in other bigger cities. Your city or area may have something equally fun. How about a double-decker bus? A school bus? They're both great ways to give your guests a taste of the area. Something out of the ordinary provides just a touch of whimsy that your guests will love.

Chapter 13
Two Months Out

Send the invitations
Seat your guests

✔ Send the Invitations

You can get away with mailing labels on your save-the-date cards, but it's best to handwrite or hire a calligrapher to address your invitations. Other tips:

- Don't buy stamps until after the invitation is assembled — you may be surprised by how much the invitation weighs or to learn that its shape affects the weight.

- Consider ordering custom (yes, there's that word again!) invitations on Zazzle.com to complete the cohesive design look.

- If you are sending any invitations overseas, don't forget to use airmail stamps for them. Be aware that you may not be able to stamp the response card.

There are lots of online resources that provide information on how to address invitations — but they're geared more to traditional couples, rather than same-sex couples. Sometimes, it may be confusing to figure out how to address invitations to LGBT couples, so here's a quick and easy lesson:

Outer envelope: If they are an unmarried couple, the names should be on two separate lines, in alphabetical order. For example:

Ms. Jennifer Coveney
Ms. Bernadette Smith
14 Willow Street
Boston, MA 02110
Inner envelope: *Ms. Coveney and Ms. Smith*

Outer envelope: If they are married with different last names, the names should be on the same line in alphabetical order. For example:

Ms. Jennifer Coveney and Ms. Bernadette Smith
14 Willow Street
Boston, MA 02110
Inner envelope: *Ms. Coveney and Ms. Smith*

Outer envelope: If they are married with the same last name, the names should be on the same line, in alphabetical order (based on first names). For example:

Mrs. and Mrs. Bernadette and Jennifer Coveney-Smith
14 Willow Street
Boston, MA 02110
Inner envelope: *Mrs. and Mrs. Coveney-Smith*

✔ Seat Your Guests

Hopefully, soon after your send out those invitations, you'll get a flurry of responses. It's now time to figure out how to seat your guests. Where you will place them at the tables is a matter of how formal you want your wedding to be. You have three choices:

• Free-for-all. Everyone sits where they want. Please don't do this. Chaos will ensue.

- Assign each guest to a table.

- Assign each guest to a table *and* a specific seat at that table.

If you are only assigning each guest to a table, you can do so in one of the following ways:

Escort Cards

Escort cards, or seating cards, tell each guest where to sit. These include the guest's name and table name or number. You can use one per couple if you wish, or give each person his or her own. Either is fine. An escort card will look like this:

Jessica Brown and Elizabeth Tupper

Table 12

Jessica and Elizabeth will pick up their card and look for table 12 — the card serves to "escort" them to that table. And once they are there, they can sit wherever they want, unless they see a place card.

Now, keep in mind that sometimes escort cards aren't cards at all — sometimes they are little strips of paper pinned into an apple on a table with rows of apples that have escort cards. Or they are names written on a pinwheel. Or they are little cards attached to a clothesline. You can be as creative as you like in personalizing the cards for your wedding.

Seating Chart

An alternative to a table full of cards is a seating chart. The chart can be a poster board (with your wedding colors or theme, please) listing the table names or numbers and the guests assigned to each.

If you do have a seating chart, make sure it looks great (an attractive frame will help add elegance), is big enough to read, is in a centrally located place, and won't cause a traffic jam.

Table Names

In the escort-card example, I used a table number but you can consider using table names to further personalize your wedding. Names do make it a little harder for the caterer to stay organized, but of course they are more fun.

Table names are typically themed. I've had clients use things like bodies of water, favorite vacation destinations, historic landmarks, baseball teams, and so on. Take your pick and have fun!

Place Cards

Place cards are the cards at each place setting that tell guests which seat belongs to them. Guests will then sit in their assigned seat. Cards are most often placed above the plate, facing outward.

Note: Bear in mind that your caterer may ask you to use place cards. For example, if you have requested that your guests preselect an entrée, your caterer may require that you indicate (on a place card) which entrée each guest requested. Note that not all caterers require this; some will ask guests which entrée they chose.

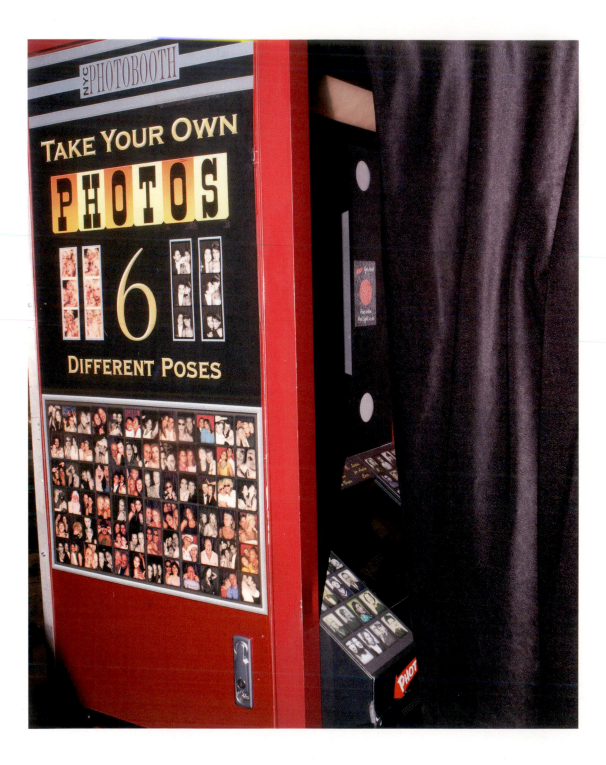

Chapter 14
One Month Out

Pop a lot of other questions
Print!
Create your wedding-day packing list
Plan and review your payment schedule
The wedding schedule
Relax

✔ Pop a Lot of Other Questions

About a month prior to your wedding, you and your partner should sit down and write down the answers to the following questions:

- Do you have any guests with disabilities or special needs?

- Are there any divorces, deaths, etc., which you should know about so as not to embarrass anyone?

- Will there be a printed program for the ceremony? Who is making this?

- Whom are you designating to distribute the program at the wedding?

- Do you want a rehearsal? If yes, then when?

- Will any drinks be passed around before the ceremony? If yes, what kinds?

- It is important to you that the ceremony start on time? What's the latest you want to start?

- Will you require ushers? Whom are you designating for this?

- Do you want any reserved seating? If so, do you want any special kinds of reserved signs? Who will provide them?

- Is there a certain side you want families and friends to sit on?

- Do you have any restrictions (e.g., no photos taken during ceremony, no confetti)?

- When do you want music to be played during the ceremony? What will the processional song be? What song will be played for the recessional?

- Whom are you designating to pin personal flowers?

- Where do you want personal flowers to be delivered?

- Do you plan to have a receiving line? When?

- Do you want any special formal photos taken (e.g., group shots, parents, etc.)?

- Do you want table names or numbers or something else?

- Do you want a sweetheart table or head table for the couple?

- Do you want any introductions to be made when the newlyweds and bridal party arrive for dinner? If yes, by whom?

- Do you want any announcements made (for first dance, cake cutting, etc.)? If yes, then when? And by whom?

- Do you want to have any special dances (first dance, father-daughter, etc.)? Who will be dancing? What song will accompany each dance? Who will give the toasts? When will they be given?

- Will there be a bouquet and/or garter toss? If yes, then when?

- Whom are you designating to transport gifts to your hotel room or home? Whom are you designating to transport floral arrangements from the ceremony to the reception?

- Where do you want flowers from the ceremony placed at the reception site?

- Whom are you designating to transport floral arrangements from the reception to your hotel room or home?

- When do you want the cake cut? Who will announce this? Do you have a special knife and server?

- Whom are you designating to transport leftover liquor, if applicable?

- Whom are you designating to distribute checks and tips?
- Do you want any personal touches in the venue's restrooms (flowers, votives, rose petals)?

Use the answers to each question to build out a task list. For example, if you haven't thought about ushers, add that to your list of things to do!

✔ Print!

If you haven't already done so, this is the time to get all materials for the ceremony and reception printed! We've already discussed seating charts, escort cards, place cards, and more — but you may still be scrambling around with RSVPs. Don't get distracted and forget to print all these items. Also, remember to print ceremony programs, table-name or table-number signs, and table menus now, too!

✔ Create Your Wedding-Day Packing List

The wedding-day packing list is a big little detail. Both of you should create it, and one of you should be responsible for checking that everything on the list makes it into the bag. Keep updating the list. You'll need this or you'll go crazy on the days leading up to your wedding.

Emergency Kit

If you hired a wedding coordinator, you won't have to worry about this because coordinators are all trained to carry emergency kits. If you didn't, take notes and head to CVS, because it's time to stock up on some emergency items. These are just some of the bare essentials:

- first-aid kit: A travel-sized kit is fine, but you should make sure there's one onsite. Check with the venue's event coordinator or with your caterer, and if they don't have a first-aid kit, buy one yourself.

- Advil, Tylenol, and antacid tablets: for aches, pains, and upset bellies (again, just in case)

- hairspray/hair gel

- tissues

- deodorant

- small mirror

- plenty of extra bobby pins

- breath mints

- clear nail polish for pantyhose runs and last-minute touch-ups

- shoeshine sponge

- sewing kit (make sure there's plenty of black and white thread)

- extra pair of black socks/nylons

- extra copy of the phone numbers and contact names of all vendors and wedding-party members

- extra copy of the wedding-day timeline

- extra copy of directions to the ceremony and reception sites

This is one of those tasks that doesn't need to be done at the last minute. If you're three months out from your wedding day and looking for a project, this is a good one to take care of.

✔ Plan and Review Your Payment Schedule

Most wedding vendors collect their final payments within 30 days of the wedding. Some require payment the night of the event, and some a week or more before. Make out a payment schedule so no one gets left out and you can rest more easily. And don't forget to budget for tips.

But, before tipping anyone, check carefully to see what is included in the bill . . . limo companies, caterers, and venues providing valet and coat check services may already have a line item for gratuities!

Tips on Tipping

Caterers: Look for a gratuity line item for both the service staff and the bartender. If it's not included, leave $35 to $60 per server and for the catering manager, and 15 to 20 percent of the bar bill for the bartender(s)

Limo driver: Tip him or her 20 percent of the bill

Musicians: Tip each musician $25 or more

DJ: Tip the DJ 15 percent of his or her fee, if it's not his or her own company

Hair and makeup: Tip the stylists 20 percent of their fees

Valet: Tip the valets $1 per car

Coat check: Coat checkers should receive 50¢ to $1 per coat

Though it's not necessary to tip the following people, you may want to do so if they've provided exceptional service:

- the photographer/videographer
- the floral designer or delivery person
- the wedding planner
- the cake-delivery person

✔ The Wedding Schedule

On the next three pages is a sample schedule from a real wedding. If you don't have a wedding coordinator who will create a schedule for you, I'd suggest going through the exercise of creating a schedule yourself. It's important to make sure that neither you (nor your friends or family) is in charge of these tasks on your wedding day. Hopefully, you'll have a day-of coordinator or a competent venue manager who can handle these tasks.

Your vendors should each receive a copy of this schedule so they can be aware of who is doing what and when. The staff at your venue should also receive a copy.

TIME	TASK	WHO
9:30 a.m.	Hair and makeup for Jess, Heather, Jennifer, Joanna, and others at the Marriott Copley Place Hotel, 110 Huntington Avenue	Jess, Heather, Jennifer, Joanna, lots of others
3:00 p.m.	Setup begins, tasks to include: • Set up tables, chairs (fruitwood chiavari, provided by Exchange Conference Center), and linens (lime twist, white napkins on dinner tables; purple twist on all other tables, provided by ECC) according to diagram • Brides have sweetheart table in window • Set up floral and candles (votives provided by ECC) • Set up restroom baskets with candles (provided by 14 Stories) • Set up 3 high cocktail tables outside (purple twist) • Set up 3 low cocktail tables outside (purple twist) • Set up escort-card clothesline • Set up typewriter guest-book table • Set up DJ booth in back-left corner • Set up paper lanterns • Set up photobooth in foyer • Set up aisle runner • Indicate that first row is reserved • Personal flowers to be left at ECC	Bornadette and catering staff, Boston Uplights, Kelly Prizel, Spruce
3:30 p.m.	• Brides arrive at ECC and receive bouquets • Kelly Prizel photographs brides finishing getting ready, walking on pier and at end of pier	Kelly, Jess, Heather
4:00 p.m.	First bus leaves Copley Marriott and goes to ECC with wedding party and families	Ritchie Bus
4:00 p.m.	• DJ Mocha arrives for setup, including speakers for outside patio area • Lamington Cake is delivered by Melita Fiore	DJ Mocha Melita Fiore
4:15 p.m.	• Those in group portraits arrive at park. Kate to pin flowers for Jess's side; Tony to pin flowers for Heather's side — confirm since they are not in the groups • Formal group portraits taken by Kelly in and around ECC and the park across from Seaport Hotel Groups to include: 1. Heather and Jess 2. Heather 3. Jess	Kelly, Kate, Tony, those in the groups

TIME	TASK	WHO
4:15 p.m.	4. Heather and her attendants Anthony, Robert, Crystal, and Michele 5. Jess and her attendants Becky, Liz, Bella, Millie 6. Heather with her mum Karen and stepdad Jim 7. Heather with her dad Scott and grammy Norma 8. Jess with her mum Molly and dad Brian 9. Jess with Anne and Ken 10. All of the above 11. Heather and Jess and both sets of parents 12. All attendants 13. Heather and Jess with all attendants 14. Heather and Jess with all of Heather's side 15. Heather and Jess with all of Jess's side **NOTE: Grammy may need a wheelchair or a walker**	Kelly, Kate, Tony, those in the groups
4:30 p.m.	Bus returns to Marriott and departs with second group	
4:45 p.m.	• Greta and Gretchen introduce themselves to me to distribute programs • Dustin and Emery introduce themselves to me to prepare to usher	Greta, Gretchen Dustin, Emery
5:00 p.m.	• Guests begin arriving at ECC; mimosas (made with Mionetto Prosecco Brut D.o.c.) and sparkling water available • DJ Mocha to start playing prelude music • Programs distributed; Dustin instructs guests not to walk on the runner	ECC staff DJ Mocha Greta, Gretchen, Dustin, Emery
5:30 p.m.	• DJ Mocha to announce, "Can you all please take your seats so we can begin the ceremony?" • DJ plays processional song "Here Comes the Sun" (acoustic guitar version) for the wedding party Processional order: • Jess's Best Woman, Becky, walks down the aisle and takes her place on the left • Heather's Man of Honor, Anthony, walks down the aisle and takes his place on the right • Liz walks down the aisle and takes her place next to Becky • Crystal walks down the aisle and takes her place next to Anthony • Bella walks down the aisle and takes her place next to Liz • Michele walks down the aisle and takes her place next to Crystal • Millie walks down the aisle and takes her place next to Bella • Robert walks down the aisle and takes his place next to Michele • Switch music to "Canon in D" for the brides • Jess goes before Heather with Brian and Molly; Heather last with Scott and Jim	Bernadette, Jess, Heather, Kezia, DJ Mocha, wedding party, Brian, Molly, Scott, Jim

TIME	TASK	WHO
6:00 p.m.	Ceremony concludes with "In My Life" by the Beatles Brides escape for 5–10 minutes and ECC staff brings them drinks and food	DJ to play ECC staff
6:05 p.m.	Guests move outside, hors d'oeuvres passed; bar open (beer and wine only: Villa Maria Sauv Blanc; Snoqualmie Chard; Banrock Shiraz; Harbortown P.N.; Harpoon IPA; Sam Adams Lager; Corona Light)	ECC staff
7:00 p.m.	Staff encourages guests to come inside for dinner	Bernadette, ECC staff
7:10 p.m.	• Guests seated (salad course is preset) • Jess and Heather held back by Bernadette • Upon sitting, DJ announces, "The brides would like to say a few words" and they make their thank-you remarks	Bernadette, DJ, Jess, Heather
7:30 p.m.	• Buffet opens • No tableside wine	ECC staff
8:15 p.m.	DJ to announce toasts: 1. Jess's sister Becky 2. Heather's brother Robert 3. Jess's dad Brian 4. Friend Abby	DJ 1. Jess's sister Becky 2. Heather's brother Robert 3 Jess's dad Brian 4. Friend Abby
8:30 p.m.	DJ to announce, "The photobooth in the hallway is now open"	Kelly, DJ
8:45 p.m.	• DJ to announce cake cutting to the song "Love Serenade" by the Waifs — no special cake knife/server • DJ to announce first dance: "I'd like to now welcome the newlyweds Jessica and Heather to the dance floor for their first dance as a married couple" to the song "Can't Help Falling in Love" by Ingrid Michaelson	DJ, Jess, Heather
9:00 p.m.	Cake is cut and dessert station is open in bar area	ECC staff
10:00 p.m.	• Sparklers lit outside by Abby and Kari to lead off the celebration • First bus leaves	Abby, Kari
10:10 p.m.	DJ to announce: "Last call for the photobooth"	DJ
11:00 p.m.	• Wedding ends; guests can help themselves to flowers • Breakdown ensues • Second bus leaves	All hands on deck

✔ Relax

Try to relax. Really. Your wedding day is going to absolutely fly by! That five- to six-hour party is over in an instant. And honestly, the ceremony is the most important part, so if some things go wrong (and they always do), just enjoy the fact that you are finally married. That's what it's all about. Try to ensure that the last few weeks leading up to the big day aren't insane for you by asking for help, delegating, and taking some quiet time alone, just the two of you.

Chapter 15
Your Lives Together

Protect your family: legally
After the vows

Congratulations! The deed is done! The knot is tied! The threshold is crossed! And off you go into the first day of the rest of your lives. It's an exciting time for any couple. But before you get too excited, there's some boring but necessary paperwork I highly recommend you take care of . . .

I'm a big fan of making sure that your lesbian family is protected. Once you're married, be aware that your marriage may not be recognized when you travel or even within your own state.

✔ Protect Your Family: Legally

Your first step is to hire an attorney knowledgeable in LGBT issues, especially estate-planning documents. While basic estate planning, involving simple joint ownership of assets, may solve some problems and avoid costly, time-consuming probate issues, estate planning for same-sex couples requires additional care. Transfers of property to an opposite-sex spouse are fully exempted from both federal estate and gift taxes, but since the IRS uses the federal definition of marriage, this exemption does not apply to same-sex couples.

Even if property is held jointly, the IRS includes the entire value of the property in the estate of the first owner to die, unless the surviving owner can provide evidence of contribution to the acquisition of the property; this issue does not exist for married opposite-sex couples.

You need to take extra steps to protect your family. Here are the types of documents that you should have drawn up. It's important to have these documents prepared by an attorney who specializes in family law and who can speak directly to you about legal protections for same-sex families.

Wills

Wills, generally considered relatively simple tools for distributing an estate's assets, can also define relationships, present evidence of intent, direct guardianship, and much more. Wills for same-sex spouses need not be dramatically different from the wills of heterosexual spouses, but they can provide special protections. Having a will in place should be a priority for any same-sex couple, young or old.

Health Care Proxies

We have all heard horror stories about how same-sex spouses are excluded from decisions about a spouse's care, treated like strangers by medical professionals, and prevented from visiting a spouse in the hospital by the spouse's blood relatives. A health care proxy is a legal document written to clearly ensure this does not happen to your family and is something you should bring with you every time you travel.

Durable Power of Attorney

Like all couples, same-sex couples want to act as one: to be able to represent one another and make decisions on each other's behalf. For same-sex couples, however, there is the added importance of recognition across state lines. Even if a couple is married in states that have legalized same-sex marriage, transacting business beyond those state lines on behalf of a same-sex spouse may not be possible without a valid Durable Power of Attorney (DPOA).

Jen and I got all our ducks in a row and filed all of these documents with the help of a fantastic attorney who specializes in protecting same-sex families. While it is an extra step, the peace of mind these documents provide (especially when you have children) is priceless. The information contained above was reprinted with permission from our attorney (and former client!), Claire DeMarco.

✔ After the Vows

Getting married is a huge step in any relationship, and as a pretty recent newlywed myself, I can say with confidence that you're going to love being married! For me and Jen, being married just made sense. Being together is the most natural thing in the world.

After our wedding, we went on a honeymoon and came back and crashed. We crashed hard! My life as a wedding planner is pretty intense about eight months a year, and our own wedding fell smack dab in the middle of typical wedding season, so I was exhausted from planning my own — and other people's — weddings. Our honeymoon in Aruba was exactly what we needed.

But then, we experienced what many couples experience — post-wedding blues. If you think about it, there's so much anticipation prior to your big day. You may have the weight of the world on your shoulders. Wedding talk may dominate your conversations at work, with friends, and with your partner. Now that the wedding's over, what's there to talk about?! I'm kidding, of course, but for some there does tend to be a letdown after all the hustle and bustle of wedding planning. That's exactly what we experienced. But it was only temporary. So don't worry if you experience something similar. It will pass — and you'll get on with enjoying life as a married couple.

Next Steps

You know the rhyme, "first comes love, then comes marriage, then comes the baby in the baby carriage." For same-sex couples, as weddings are normalized and become more common, this is what happens with many families. We fall in love, we marry (now legally, in a growing number of states), and then some of us have kids. It's exciting. But it also brings more responsibilities.

Money management is a key concern for couples, straight and LGBT. I recommend that you find a financial planner who is attuned to the needs of same-sex couples and their families, so that you get investment advice that addresses your specific needs, from someone comfortable working with the LGBT community. Planning ahead can be a solid investment in your future!

Jen and I now have a wild little boy named Patrick and another one possibly on the way. This is the path we chose and we love our life. We hope you'll find much happiness, too, as you begin your journey as a married couple!

Acknowledgments

When I met my wife, my company was merely three years old and going through a mild rough patch. I was debating whether to chug along or close up shop. Jen believed in me and in the mission of 14 Stories, and gave me the inspiration and push to grow my little company into something extraordinary. This book is for Jen, my great love.

Thanks also to Sellers Publishing for believing in me and in this important material. Thanks to Mark Chimsky for being a patient and thoughtful editor, to Sellers Publishing's Managing Editor Mary Baldwin for her production expertise, and to proofreader Amy Chamberlain for all her help. But I wouldn't have connected with Sellers if it weren't for the lovely Marilyn Allen, from Allen O'Shea Literary Agency, who found me and has been a great ally. Thank you, Marilyn.

Thanks to the photographers whose beautiful work is seen in these pages — particularly Katje Hempel, with whom I've collaborated on many weddings.

But above all, thanks to my clients, the hundreds of LGBT couples from around the world who have entrusted 14 Stories with their precious wedding plans. Thanks for sharing your own stories with me and trusting in us to bring your story to life through your wedding. I am thrilled to now count many of you as personal friends.

Appendix 1: Important Stats

In 2010 and 2011, the 14 Stories Gay Wedding Institute conducted the largest survey ever of engaged and newlywed same-sex couples. Here are some of the notable findings:

- 75% of 500+ respondents were lesbian couples

- 68% of respondents were 24–40 years old

- 43% were 32–50 years old

- 84% are having a legal marriage ceremony, not just a commitment ceremony

- 82% of those who live in a state where same-sex marriage is not legal will travel to legally marry

- 67% are paying for the wedding entirely themselves

- Only 16% of same-sex couples do not receive any emotional support from their parents

- 63% have the emotional support of both sets of parents

- 64% of same-sex couples have a wedding party; 36% have no attendants

- 97% of respondents reported that it was very or somewhat important for them to legally marry

- 74% found it very or somewhat important to hire LGBT-owned businesses

- 78% found it very or somewhat important to hire wedding vendors that specifically advertise to the LGBT community

- 85% found it very or somewhat important to hire wedding vendors with LGBT-inclusive language

- 81% found it very or somewhat important to hire wedding vendors with LGBT-inclusive photos

- 82% found it very or somewhat important to hire wedding vendors that have specifically been trained about LGBT weddings

- 92% of same-sex couples do not have their ceremony in a place of worship

- 30% of same-sex wedding ceremonies have all of the guests standing; 13% have two aisles; and 57% have one central aisle

- 30% of lesbian couples enter the ceremony down two aisles or from two different directions

- In 42% of lesbian couples, both wore a wedding gown; in 12%, both wore a suit or tux, and in 46%, one wore a dress and the other wore a suit

- 91% of lesbian couples get ready together before the wedding

Appendix 2: Resources

Same-Sex Wedding-Planning Resources
- 14Stories.com
- Gay.Weddings.com
- GayWeddings.com
- EquallyWed.com
- AVoteandaVow.com

General Wedding-Planning Resources
- Pinterest.com
- Etsy.com
- WeddingChicks.com
- WeddingWire.com

Do-It-Yourself Project Resources
- AlbumBoutique.com
- DIYBride.com
- MarthaStewartWeddings.com
- WeddingChicks.com

Green Weddings
- GreenBrideGuide.com
- Eco-BeautifulWeddings.com

Invitations
- GayWeddings.com
- TwoPaperDolls.com
- LadyfingersLetterpress.com
- OutVite.com
- WeddingPaperDivas.com

Wedding Accessories
- KateParkerDesigns.com (welcome bags)
- Beau-Coup.com (favors and other decorative items)
- Etsy.com (all things handcrafted)
- IDoEngravables.com (as a guest book substitute)
- ModernKetubah.com (for the foundation covenant and *ketubahs*)
- PalomasNest.com (for ring-bearer bowls and napkin rings)
- TheGarterGirl.com (for stylish wedding garters)

Legal
- GLAD.org
- LambdaLegal.org

Advocacy
- Human Rights Campaign, HRC.org
- National Center for Lesbian Rights, NCLRights.org
- National Gay and Lesbian Task Force, NGLTF.org

Media
- GLAAD, www.GLAAD.org

Index

Page numbers in *italic* indicate tips and useful wedding planning forms.